Military Education Benefits for College

A Comprehensive Guide for Military Members, Veterans, and Their Dependents

David J. Renza and
Lieutenant Colonel Edmund J. Lizotte (Ret.)

Savas Beatie
California and New York

© 2010 by David J. Renza and Edmund J. Lizotte

All rights reserved. No part of this publication may be reproduced, stored in a retrieval system, or transmitted, in any form or by any means, electronic, mechanical, photocopying, recording, or otherwise, without the prior written permission of the publisher.

Cataloging-in-Publication Data is available from the Library of Congress.

First edition, first printing
ISBN-13: 978-1-932714-79-1

SB
Published by
Savas Beatie LLC
521 Fifth Avenue, Suite 1700
New York, NY 10175

Editorial Offices:

Savas Beatie LLC
P.O. Box 4527
El Dorado Hills, CA 95762
Phone: 916-941-6896
(E-mail) editorial@savasbeatie.com

Savas Beatie titles are available at special discounts for bulk purchases in the United States by corporations and other organizations. For more details, contact Special Sales, P.O. Box 4527, El Dorado Hills, CA 95762. You may e-mail us about your needs at sales@savasbeatie.com, or you may visit our website at www.savasbeatie.com for additional information.

Front Cover: Mathias Wilson

Interior artwork by David Sanangelo

Proudly printed and bound in the United States of America.

To my family and friends, in particular my parents who have been extremely supportive of me in my pursuit of success.

And to those who have served our country and those who continue to serve with honor, protecting our peace and the liberties we enjoy.

And to my grandfathers who served in World Wars I and II, and my good friends from the 143rd FSB, who were an honor and pleasure to serve with.

— *David J. Renza*

This book is dedicated to all the young men and women, who selflessly choose to take up the mantle of Soldier, Marine, Sailor, or Airman and defend our way of life; and to those who support their servicemember.

I also dedicate this book to my Father, who started our family tradition of service by serving our country during WWII; my brother, who continued the tradition while serving our country in Vietnam; and to my sons, who served our country during OIF/OEF and who are now using their GI Bill benefits to earn their college degrees.

— *Lt. Col. Edmund J. Lizotte, (Ret.)*

Contents

Introduction / Acknowledgments
vi

Chapter 1: Why Going to College is the Right Choice
1

Chapter 2: How Do I Begin?
12

Chapter 3: What Degree Program is Right for Me?
16

Chapter 4: How Do I Select a School?
35

Chapter 5: The College Admissions Process
61

Chapter 6: How Do I Pay for College?
86

Chapter 7: What Can I Expect as a College Student?
117

Chapter 8: Serving While Studying
129

Conclusion: Congratulations—You Did It! Now What?
160

Appendices: Checklists and Questions to Ask
165

References
172

Index
173

Website List
180

Introduction

We have utilized our education benefits to help shape our own careers inside and outside of the military. Our hope now, since you are holding this book in your hands, is that we can help you do the same.

Military Education Benefits for College will assist you each step of the way by helping to remove some of the confusion surrounding education benefits and the college experience as a whole for service connected students (SCS). Some people approach school with apprehension, while others are simply paraylized by indecision with the thought of preparing for higher education. Obtaining a college education for some service connected students is about as scary as a new recruit going through basic training (yes, we have been told that!). It should not be, and doesn't have to be this way, however. The college experience—regardless of whether you are in the military, a veteran, or are a dependent of someone who is—should be and can be a rewarding and engaging experience. Like anything worthwhile, it will be difficult and challenging at times, and perhaps downright frustrating at others, but ultimately it will help you achieve your personal and professional goals. And for many of you, it will change your lives in ways you never thought imaginable.

A words about this book. First, it will offer you reassurance that you have made the right decision by choosing to begin—or for some of you, complete—your education. The dynamics of the changing industries and technology mean that earning your degree is now <u>a requirement</u>. You can not longer afford to leave your time in service or let your education benefits run out without an education to show for it.

Next, we will help you get started with the entire process. We will walk you through the admissions process and make certain that you are armed with all of the paperwork you will need to complete your college admission as quickly and painlessly as possible. We will also help you choose a school and a degree program that's right for you. Choosing a solid program will help ensure you that you can utilize your certificate or degree with the best possibility for positive results, whether you are looking for promotion in your current career or within your branch of the service, or a new opportunity altogether. Choosing the right school will ensure that pursuing that degree or certificate is as rewarding an experience as it can be, and makes it more likely that you, the service connected student, have the support you need to be successful.

We will also help you through the payment process. The majority of people who join the military do so with the intent of using their education benefits, but few know exactly what's out there for them or where to find access to them. This book sheds light on that thorny subject.

Finally, we will walk you through the college experience. What does it take to be a successful student? How do you get acclimated to the college experience? Our advice contained in this book is based upon our combined experiences from real case scenarios we have dealt with in miltitary-related admissions. We realized that acadamia is an entirely new world for many of you; trust us, it is completely different from anything you may have encountered in the service. Finally, we will help you consider some decisions you may come across when you are finished with your education. So whether you have never been to college before, have gone and dropped or transferred out, or just want to explore your options, there is something in this book for everyone with a military-related background.

Although there are other books available, most are out of date and only touch lightly on too many important areas. Other information can be found on the Internet, but can you trust it? Is it up to date? And do you have the time and energy to search and find quality material from literally dozens of websites, and then integrate it for your own personal use?

We wrote *Military Education Benefits for College* with these thoughts in mind and for two key reasons. First, our job experience is the college admissions process because both of us are admissions counselors. We deal daily with the educational-related challenges that military students face. Not only do we both work with military, veteran, and dependent student populations, but we also worked with recruiting and retention during our active-duty military careers and have used—and are still using—our own military education benefits.

Second, we believed it was important that we write this book because we feel very strongly about one important theme you will hear over and over: *If you are able to pursue your education now, get it done!*

Don't wait, don't pause, don't deviate from the goal you have set for yourself, whether it's a training license to drive a truck or a bachelor's degree in psychology, a certificate in human resources management, or a doctorate in psychology. Don't hesitate in getting started and see it through all the way, if only for this one simple reason: *If not now, when?*

Especially if you are young or still in your early years in the military, putting off starting college often seems an attractive choice. After all, you are learning your military occupation and getting used to your duty station. You won't be retired for perhaps two or more decades. After that, you tell yourself, you can find the time to use your GI Bill benefits. By that time (or before) you will have a family to worry about and many other things that come along with age and experience. If you have ten reasons now why it is not a good time to go to school, the odds are that you will have 100 good reasons why it won't be a good time in the future.

The road might be long, but we promise to help you navigate it and, like your military career, with hard work, dedication, and perseverance you will succeed. *We* can't guarantee you success—that part is up to *you*. However, we can show you from our own personal experiences as students and admissions counselors for Service Connected Students that if you follow our guidelines and put forth your best effort, you will have an excellent chance of achieving your ultimate goal of a college education.

And when that day comes, you will be able to proudly stand up in front of your family, friends, co-workers or unit, and beam with pride in knowing that you just helped improve your most important weapon—your mind!

Acknowledgments

We would like to take this opportunity to thank many wonderful people for their assistance, advice, and support.

First and foremost we thank our publisher Savas Beatie, which publishes a deep and varied line of military-related titles. A special thanks to two individuals in particular: Marketing Director Sarah Keeney for her tireless devotion to making sure our message gets out to as many people as possible, and to Managing Director Theodore P. Savas for sharing our vision from the start. Ted realized the critical need for a book like this, and put a lot on the line to make this happen.

The staff at Post University deserves a special nod of thanks, in particular Drs. Kenneth Zirkle and Thomas Sampf for offering their advice and support from before we wrote a single word and for allowing us to use relevant forms for examples in this book. Francis Mulgrew and Veronica Marrero allowed us the time necessary to complete the writing process. Thanks also to Barry Zucker and Ryan Tiscia for the photographs, Tom Van Stone for technological advice, and Post University student Chris Williams for setting up the blog and website.

The Department of Veterans Affairs and the various Education Support Offices answered our questions, and in particular helped keep us informed about ongoing changes to the post-9/11 Bill and assisted in producing what we hope will be the best resource for Service Connected Students.

Many Service Connected Students volunteered their time to help us, in particular those from the Waterbury, Connecticut, Military Recruiting Station, 395th CSSB in Iraq, and the Connecticut, New Hampshire, and Tennessee Army National Guard members who were willing to be photographed and interviewed. They shared their stories and experiences with us and embody the true meaning of Chapter 8—Serving While Studying!

Finally, we would like to thank the following individuals for helping make this vision a reality in the formative stages: David SanAngelo, for his amazing talent in bringing Sergeant Student and Colonel Classroom to life; Carol Renza, Anthony Gallo, Esq., and Peter Zezima, CPA, for their business advice; and a special thank you to Bill Kelly and Dr. Michael Alfano from the University of Connecticut's Neag School of Education for helping us recognize the need for this book through our experiences.

CHAPTER 1

Why Going to College is the Right Choice

"Destiny is not a matter of chance, it is a matter of choice;
it is not a thing to be waited for, it is a thing to be achieved."

— William Jennings Bryan

The First Step

If you have purchased this book, chances are you have made the decision to begin attending school for the first time or, for some of you, to continue with some unfinished business. Making the decision to explore the possibility of education can be a daunting task. Consider the seemingly endless amount of paperwork and research you will have to do in the very near future—and we're not even talking about the classroom! We want to commend you for taking the first step to at least *consider* going to school and using the education benefits that are available to you.

In case you need to be reminded, you are a recipient of these benefits because you or someone close to you currently or at one point in time was an active member of the military. Your benefits weren't free. Chances are you or someone in your family had to work very hard to earn these benefits, and at some point in time you or someone close to you endured parting ways with a loved one. In the case of survivor benefits, someone made the ultimate sacrifice for you to obtain the benefits you are about to use.

Either way, let there be no doubt in your mind that these benefits were *earned* and are offered to you with the reverence and gratitude of a grateful nation. Consider them a small token of gratitude for whatever sacrifices you or someone close to you made to obtain them. Your only obligation is to use them wisely for whatever self-improvement you seek.

THE BIG IDEA! *You've decided to take that first step toward your educational goals. Great work! Soon, you will see how obtaining the degree or certification you desire will offer you a wealth of opportunities you never thought possible!*

The Most Important Question

For those of you who are entering or re-entering the world of education, we have just one question for you: *why?* There are a number of reasons why it is to your benefit to pursue your college education.

Why Furthering Your Education Is So Important

If you are already reading this book, you have more than likely realized that education is an important way to get ahead in today's world. If you still are not 100% certain why you are here and why education is so important, we are not here to twist your arm. But we can offer you some eye-opening facts on why choosing to further your education makes good sense.

For starters, open your local newspaper. Look at the business section. Notice all of the companies downsizing and outsourcing to other countries also while laying off countless workers. Jobs that were once plentiful in America are disappearing. The economic downturn has affected greatly the job market in ways few people could have imagined even just a few short years ago. Unemployment rates continue to rise, and when that happens, the cream rises to the top with it. Of course, if you are not holding a special piece of paper in your hands, you have a much greater chance of being left on the outside looking in.

Now, scan the classifieds. Look for what jobs are being offered. Not only are there fewer to choose from, but the chances are you will see another big change. You will notice that the majority of them are looking for a certificate or degree of some sort even to be considered for the position. Even as little as five or ten years ago, some of those jobs didn't require any special schooling at all. Now, it's hard to find even entry-level jobs that do not require an associate's degree or certification of some sort *at a minimum.*

LISTEN UP—IMPORTANT POINT! Getting an education is important, and if you are thinking about another career or advancing in the one you are currently in, a degree can only help you. Not only are employers expecting more today, but the competition for jobs is extremely high. The following data was compiled to confirm that American adults are beginning to value college educations more than ever. Read on . . .

* * *

Adults 25 and Older With College Education, 1990. Source: U.S. Department of Education

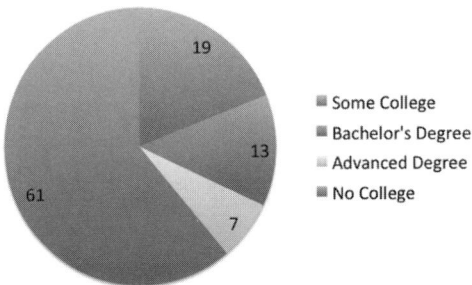

Adults 25 and Older With College Education, 2000. Source: U.S. Department of Education

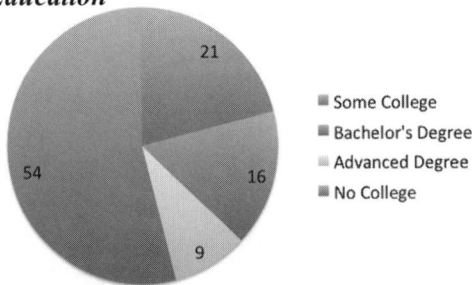

This transformation is partially the result of a continued progression of our culture and workforce from agriculture- and factory-based, to jobs demanding a higher skill qualification for workers. Additionally, this is also a reflection on the increased value of a degree for the employer and the workforce alike. The increase of students with some college-level education in the workforce between 1990 and 2000 of about seven percent (7%) means that by the time data for the new decade becomes available, for the first time in our nation's history we could easily see a majority of adult workers with at least *some* college education. What does this mean to you? Your competition for career advancement or promotion just got a lot more intense.

And if that weren't enough proof you made the right decision, check this out:

Average Annual Salaries for Adults. Source: U.S. News and World Report

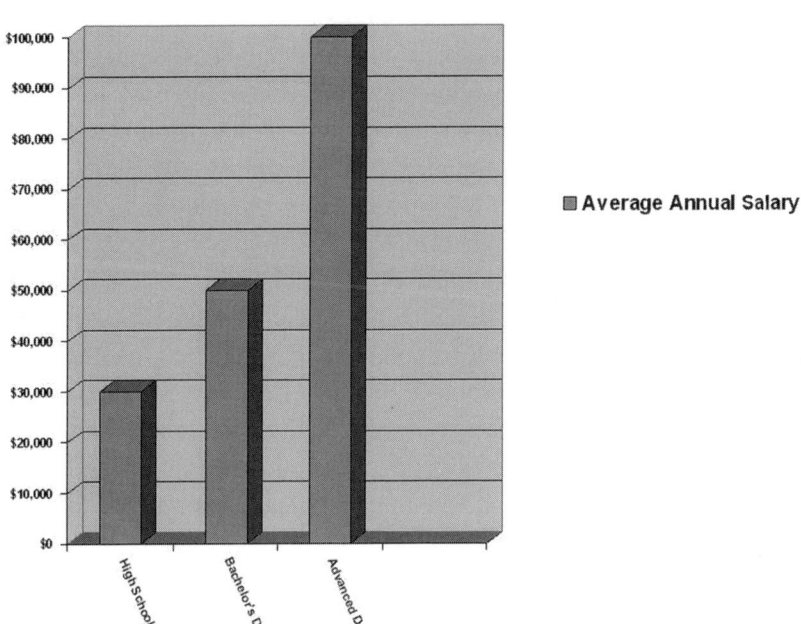

According to the *U.S. News and World Report*, a leading authority on higher education, workers with a bachelor's degree on average make an additional $20,000 per year than workers with just a high school diploma. Not enough? Workers with an advanced professional degree, such as an MBA or law degree, can make upwards of $100,000 per year. That's a whopping $70,000 per year more than workers without a college education on their resume! But the most important piece of data in that report was that, with the costs of a college education, particularly at the graduate and professional school level, creeping into six-digit territory, the chances of a student seeing a return on the investment in the short term is slim.

Some of you may be confused at why we consider that piece of data to be the most important. Doesn't that money spent up front mean anything in the equation of how much you stand to make? As surprising as this sounds, it means less than you may think.

LISTEN UP— IMPORTANT POINT!

Not one piece of that statistical data took into account any education benefits available to you as a Service Connected Service (SCS).

Each of you reading this book has a wide variety of opportunities depending upon your eligibility—from waivers and stipends to discounts, scholarships, and grants—that can help bring down college costs significantly. In some cases, obtaining a degree won't cost you a dime. Either way, you can be certain that your ability to recoup the financial benefits of your degree will happen much faster than your civilian student counterparts.

To elaborate the point of why a college education is important to you both while you are in the service and when you get out, take a look at the following side-by-side comparison chart that appears on the next page. What you see are two identical service members. Both are in the same branch of service, have achieved the same rank, are the same age, and have the same number of years of service. The difference is that SSG Student has chosen to enroll in college and earn his bachelor's degree while still serving in the military. As you can see, because of his college education, he has qualified for two more promotions than did SSG Soldier. Why? Because each branch of the service provides for administrative promotion points for earning college degrees. The major difference comes when they both reach retirement and separate from the military. SSG Student will be able to get a job that will pay him almost twice what SSG Soldier will be able to get with just a high school degree—even though he has the same amount of experience as SSG Student. Why? Because having that bachelor's degree allows SSG Student to leverage both his experience and his education to demand a higher paying salary!

SSG Soldier		SSG Student	
Rank	E-6	Rank	E-6
Age	24	Age	24
Years of Service	6	Years of Service	6
High School Diploma	YES	High School Diploma	YES
Associate's Degree	NO	Associate's Degree	YES
Attends Service NCO Schools	YES	Attends Service NCO Schools	YES
Bachelor's Degree	NO	Bachelor's Degree	YES
Promoted	1 time	Promoted	3 times
20 Year Retirement	YES	20 Year Retirement	YES
Civilian Salary at Retirement*	$37,855	Civilian Salary at Retirement*	$62,085

Based on average salaries for adults. Source: U. S. News and World Report

The reason we are asking you *why* you want to go to college is not to inject you with self-doubt or second-guessing, but rather to give you the reason to stick with it once you start! It will be the most important thing that will keep you going when you are running straight from your job that ends at 5:00 p.m. to class uptown that starts at 6:00 p.m., when you are up at 2:30 in the morning studying while your spouse is fast asleep, or when you have a deadline for a paper fast approaching while your friends attend a special event without you.

The trouble is, along the way you are going to ask yourself over and over again why you decided to go to school—maybe because of one of the above scenarios or something else. But the answer to that question will help unfailingly guide you to that awesome day when you realize that sense of pride and accomplishment that comes from wearing a cap and gown! Some of you may liken it to the day when you graduated basic training. Others may be reminded of welcoming a loved one home from a deployment to a distant land with other flag-waving well-wishers. May those warm thoughts of pleasant days ahead also provide you with the inspiration to complete your journey.

THE BIG IDEA! *Putting your own educational and personal goals in perspective will help keep you on track and help provide you with a beacon of comfort when things get tough. Believe me—they will!*

Education Benefits: You have earned them—so use them!

In gratitude for your service to our country, whether you are still in the military or you are now a veteran or retiree, you have education benefits that in most cases will pay for your entire civilian education. The sad thing about this is that not everyone who is eligible actually uses them. As a person eligible for these benefits, that makes you a ***Service***

Connected Student—hereafter referred to as an ***SCS***. An SCS is any person who is eligible for benefits as a current member of the military or former member of the military with more than 90 days of active duty service, or a dependent of an individual who is eligible for these benefits. Your determination of your eligibility was probably one of the first catalysts that prompted you to explore education in first place.

These benefits have a variety of limits in terms of cost, duration, and availability depending on many factors, to include time in service, type of service, and relationship to the service member. At a minimum, your status as an SCS enables you to have a discount on tuition offered by some institutions. Any further benefits are determined by any number of factors, including whether or not you are still an active member of the service, how long you served for (and in what capacity), and even what state you live in.

Your eligibility or potential benefits available as an SCS cannot be determined by either of the authors of this book. Instead, we will guide you in the direction of which benefits you may be eligible for, and tell you how you may be able to utilize them to fund your education. This may all sound like gibberish, but don't worry, because we will explain each of these programs in great detail in this book. You just need to realize that you, the SCS, have a great opportunity to further your education and have the majority of it, and perhaps all of it, paid for by your educational benefits.

THE BIG IDEA! *You didn't have to look far to find a good reason to go back to school. Your military education benefits available to you as an SCS will help ensure that you don't have to look far for ways to pay for your education, either!*

Plan for the Future

To drive this point home, we want you to look at a hypothetical student. Let's say we have an SCS who is a 25-year-old Staff Sergeant in the Air Force. He has been in the Air Force seven years, since his graduation from high school. His plans are to stay in the Air Force until retirement and then pursue his education. With retirement so far off, he hasn't really considered school during active duty, since he is convinced he will be in the Air Force for at least another 13 or more years.

This sounds like logical planning—except for one big thing: What if he decides, after 10 years in the service, that he has had enough of the Air Force? That means he will be leaving the Air Force without a retirement paycheck and forced to look for employment outside the service armed with little more than his Air Force experience.

Here's another thought: What if at the age of 25 our hypothetical Staff Sergeant was a single SCS with no family commitments. Suddenly, at the age of 30, he decides to have a family and puts off his own education until his children have moved on to college themselves. Then, faced with the rising costs of education for his high school and college-aged kids, he decides that, at the age of 50, it's better to pass on his education benefits than to use them for himself.

LISTEN UP—IMPORTANT POINT!

The fact of the matter is that when you are a young SCS it is difficult to see that far into the future. You can expect what will happen in the future, but you can't *predict* what will happen.

This is especially true of anyone who is an SCS still in the military. At this stage in your life, you may see things from an entirely different perspective than you will 10 or 20 years down the road. That's human nature. That's why it's imperative to act now on utilizing your military education benefits and starting and completing your educational goals.

Why Going to College is the Right Choice

When you joined the military your recruiter used your education as a recruiting tool for you to join the service. As a student right out of high school, this was probably one of the reasons you joined at the time. However, as time wore on and you got comfortable in your military career and your lifestyle, it became less and less important to you.

The sense of urgency may change as you get older, but your personal situation may change as well, making it more difficult to attend school than before. That's why it's so important to act now on your educational ambitions. Maybe at this time you may think that an opportunity will arise later for you to pursue your educational goals, but there is really no time like the present. *Carpe diem*—seize the day!

By the way, our tour guides through the education process are Sergeant Student and Colonel Classroom. Like many of you, Sergeant Student knows it's time for thinking about his future in the military, and his future after the military. He's carefully considering all of his options about school and integrating it into his busy life. With our steps outlining the process to help you along the way and some guidance from the colonel, hopefully you will have similar success pursuing your own education.

Let's get started.

THE BIG IDEA! *Taking advantage of your education benefits sooner rather than later means that you are ensuring yourself a greater chance of benefitting from them in the long run—not to mention, more of a chance you will use them, period. What are you waiting for?*

CHAPTER 2

How Do I Begin?

"Throughout the centuries there were men who took first steps down new roads armed with nothing but their own vision."

— Ayn Rand

How Do I Begin?

As with anything, the best place to start is at the beginning. Whether you have just completed basic training and your military job schooling, you have been in the military for 10 years and are now ready to start your college education, or you have separated from the military and you want to take advantage of your GI Bill benefits, starting your college education can be a daunting but not impossible task. But the process for going to college is the same for everyone, and every college has the same basic process.

In the chapters that follow, we will take you through the entire process from selecting the right school for you, choosing a degree program, and enrolling in that school. We will point out potential pitfalls and key points to keep in mind as you travel through this process. The key to success on this journey is to ask questions and not to jump hastily into a school and/or program. We will provide you with some useful tools that you can use as you start your path toward earning your college degree.

The key thing to remember is that this is a process, and as long as you follow the steps, you will achieve your goal. The diagram below illustrates the overall process and will help to guide you along your path to earning your degree.

There are a lot of steps in planning and implementing your education, and we want to make sure that you stay on track and don't miss anything along the way. To do this, we have provided a checklist to follow and mark things off as you complete them. This way, even if you are delayed from starting your college pursuits because of a deployment, civilian job, or just life demands that you put things on hold, you won't have to start from scratch and you can pick up from where you left off. The checklist can be found in *Appendix 1* near the end of the book. We strongly encourage you to carefully tear or cut the page out and put it in your file folder along with the other documents that you will need to complete your college enrollment.

Consider Your Situation

Start with yourself. As a future SCS, it's time to determine what your goals for your education are. Some things to consider:

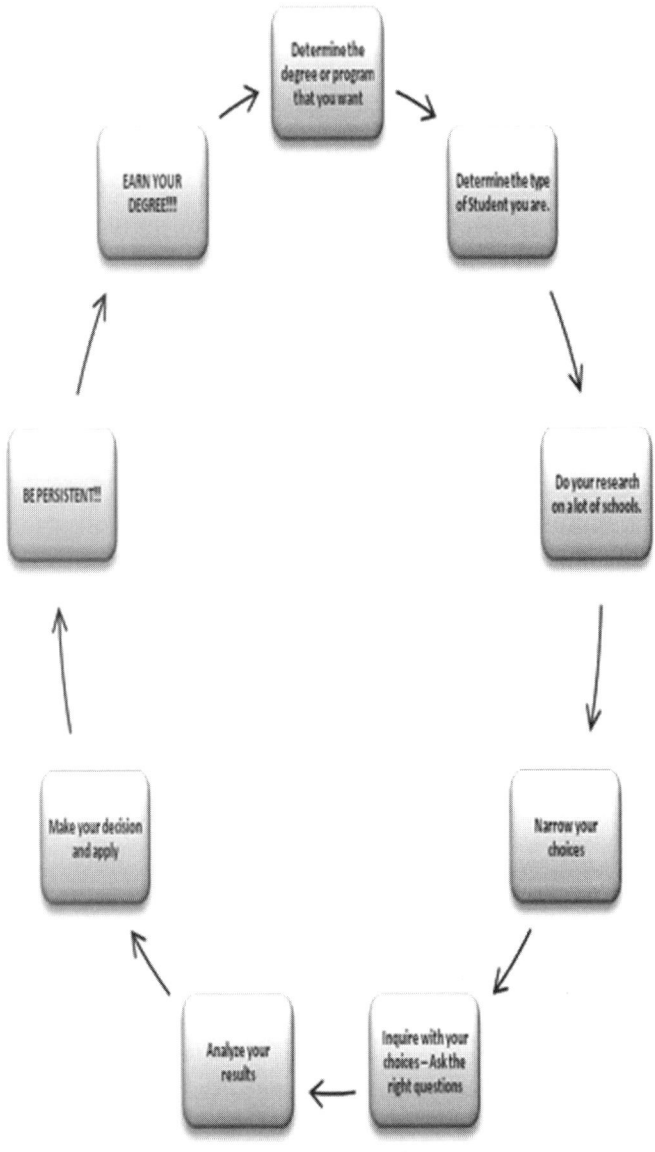

Steps in the Process

- *What type of student will you be?* Are you a professional or an older student looking to earn your degree quickly and conveniently, or are you looking for a degree at the pace of a more traditional college student?

How Do I Begin? 15

- *What type of degree plan are you seeking?* While many schools have many different degrees to offer, some specialize in particular degrees or programs.

- *What are your other plans during your education?* We all know that much like the military, life doesn't stop while we are at school. Are you physically able to attend classes? Will your change in work location or military duty station possibly force a transfer in schools? Will the possibility of starting a family force you to put your plans on hold for a semester?

Once you answer these questions, you'll have a much clearer idea of what school may be right for you.

If your goal is to become a lawyer or a college professor, you may find that you need to dedicate yourself to becoming a full-time student. You may need to change your duty status or lifestyle as a whole in order to achieve your goal. However, if your desire is to obtain a business marketing degree or a paralegal certificate, you will probably discover that you can still serve your country or work full-time while doing so because of the conveniences such programs offer most students. Regardless of the goal, the key to success is to maximize your benefits and availability to college programs. The ever-increasing amount and quality of low-residency and online programs make it possible to pursue your degree with minimal or no interaction on campus.

THE BIG IDEA! *You need to look at yourself, and at your educational goals and needs, before you begin to think where you are going to school. Taking care of this important step first will help you weigh your options and make a better decision. A wealth of opportunities you never thought were possible await you!*

CHAPTER 3

What Degree Program is Right for Me?

"There are no secrets to success. It is the result of preparation, hard work, and learning from failure."

— Gen. Colin Powell

Taking the First Steps

One of the challenges that can overcome the SCS is the inability to make a decision on a degree plan. This is understandable due to the nature of the military lifestyle. Our research has brought an interesting fact to light. Many active members of the military are advised by Education Support Specialists to enroll into Liberal Arts or General Studies degree programs because they are often very flexible, and the SCS can transfer in a great deal of military credits into many of these programs. The majority of the time, this is because the military student often does not know what he plans on doing with his or her degree, or more importantly, what the plan is after he gets out of the military. SCS who spent years moving around different occupations and bases in the military often follow various paths in their education. This can be due to changes in curriculums between the various institutions they attend or change in career or educational interests and objectives throughout their career.

LISTEN UP—IMPORTANT POINT!

The key to achieving success quickly in your military education is realizing which path you want to take—if at all possible—*before* you start attending school. This means you should look ahead to what you want to do when you get out of the military. For example, if you are in the Army as a Military Police Officer, but when you get out of the Army you have no intentions of going into Law Enforcement, then why would you want to get a Criminal Justice Degree?

The reason it's best to consider your career path before taking classes is to avoid transcripts of credits scattered in many different areas with no real definition or use—something that we see often when dealing with SCS who served on active duty. These scattered credits may look good for promotion boards that are impressed with total credits and not degrees obtained, but the sooner you focus your college credits on degree completion, the quicker you will earn opportunities at career advancement inside and outside the military and stop wasting your time in the classroom by taking several courses that don't fit into the curriculum of your ultimate degree choice.

For those of you reading this book who are sure of what you want to do, but aren't sure of your own abilities in that area of study, our suggestion is to go gently into the course work geared toward your career. Approach it as you would a fully executed mobilization. Consider your prerequisites (mathematics, social sciences, humanities) as your "support operations," and consider your courses toward your major your "fighting force." Use your first year or two of studies taking mostly prerequisites that can usually be transferred to another program if needed, and begin slowly integrating courses toward your major requirements to see if you enjoy the studies you've chosen. This way, if you decide that the career plan you chose initially isn't the right fit for you, the basic core credits you have already taken can (often) be applied toward another degree, and your specialized courses can count toward your requirements as electives in a different degree plan. Remember to choose your courses wisely: be efficient and be smart, and please use your academic advisor as your guide. If you are at all uncertain of what courses to register for next, ASK your academic advisor!

THE BIG IDEA! *Making a decision quickly about the course of study you want to pursue is key in making sure you don't waste time taking classes you don't need. If you aren't sure what you want to do with your education or what course work is right for you, choose your courses wisely and they can easily be transferred into another program.*

Types of College Degrees

Degrees tend to fall into several categories, and especially one of the following three categories: Career-oriented, Liberal Arts, or General Studies Degrees. Let's look at each one in turn.

Career-oriented degrees are those degrees that college students obtain if their goal is to go into the workforce right after graduation and they do not have any plans to attend graduate school, medical school, or law school. The following list shows some of the degree programs that would be considered career-oriented:

- Bachelor's of Science in Business Management

- Bachelor's of Science in Accounting

- Bachelor's of Science in Finance

- Bachelor's of Science in Computer Informational Systems

Liberal Arts degrees are primarily focused on imparting knowledge to the student in a variety of subject areas, like humanities (English, history), social sciences (political science, sociology), and arts (music, theater). General Studies degrees are not focused in any one particular area, but are designed to give professional skills to students in any one of a variety of fields designed to prepare students for any number of specialized careers to include: business, finance and accounting, medical administration, public service, and law enforcement. These programs tend to have classes and schedules that cater to the non-traditional student, including online students, distance-learning, and night or weekend courses.

A Liberal Arts degree for a person with an interest in a specific subject is a terrific degree to have. For one, you could turn a passion for science, ancient history, or literature into a career in education. The military has an outstanding program called "Troops-to-Teachers" that recognizes that the leadership, teaching, and learning skills you displayed on the battlefield are qualities that lend themselves well to effective teaching techniques and have a great chance of positively influencing students in the classroom, particularly in urban areas. For more details and information on Troops-To-Teachers, please go to www.proudtoserveagain.com.

While a Liberal Arts degree can also prepare veteran SCS for unique careers in fields such as journalism or archeology, keep in mind these jobs are not plentiful. What's more, with increasing competition in the job market, the odds of a military person's experience coupled with a Liberal Arts degree (or no degree at all) finding a successful career outside of education may decrease dramatically.

General Studies degrees were specifically designed to cater to the general population with no specific intend in mind. One of the first such programs was created as a response to a large student population returning home after World War II. General Dwight Eisenhower, then the President of Columbia University in New York City, saw an opportunity to cater to some of the service members he led, providing them with a convenient education that allowed them to use their new Montgomery GI Bill education benefits. Columbia's Bachelors of General Studies program became the benchmark of what are the professional degree programs of today.

LISTEN UP—IMPORTANT POINT!

A career-oriented degree with a specialization in any number of career fields may offer the SCS an opportunity to be more attractive to more employers.

What's more, career-oriented degree programs are usually designed around work schedules, offering students the opportunity to continue to work traditional jobs and military careers while earning a degree that offers the opportunity for advancement. (The format for these programs can vary from accelerated degree plans, night and weekend classes, and online schools.)

Your Military Career as College Credits?

What do an Army tank commander, a Navy corpsman, an Air Force crew chief, and Marine sniper all have in common? They all have military occupations and careers that can be evaluated for college credit in any accredited institution. While all of these examples come from different career paths, the training they received in the military can be worth college credits and will be evaluated on a case-by-case basis by almost every institution.

What Degree Program Is Right for Me?

THE BIG IDEA! *Career-oriented Studies programs typically offer courses of study that are most appealing to employers and offer effective ways to showcase your military talents in a dynamic and rewarding career. Be aware of this when choosing what type of program you enter and career field you pursue.*

While basic training often fills elective credits in areas such as physical fitness, occupation training can fill electives as well as other areas such as science and humanities. While the vast majority of occupational training rarely amounts to more than three to twelve college credits, some schools have agreements based on their curriculum in certain professional degree programs to offer college credits based on certain degree programs.

It's also important to note that some occupations often have the same training requirements and standards as civilian schools for vocational credits, and often allow you to sit for certification tests in civilian counterpart areas. For example, many vehicle engine repair specialists train to take certified mechanic exams, and army medics are now required to take the National EMT Registry exam as part of their MOS qualification—both of which can lead to civilian employment.

Regardless of which MOS you choose, make sure when you apply for colleges to have your credits evaluated by an academic advisor. As you progress throughout your military career, you take on additional skills or leadership training that can also be used for credits, so be sure your advisor is aware of any updates. Leadership development courses, such as BNCOC or ANCOC in the army, can be considered credits for classes in management and career development. Your military training is a valuable education experience that can help you even in civilian sectors, so having your transcripts reviewed is an important step.

LISTEN UP—IMPORTANT POINT!

Remember to have a copy of your transcripts and your DD-214 forms printed and ready to show your academic advisor. To obtain a transcript of your military training and qualifications, please go to the following websites:

Air Force / Air National Guard:
www.au.af.mil/au/ccaf/

Army / Army National Guard:
https://aartstranscript.army.mil/

Coast Guard:
www.uscg.mil/hq/cgi/ve/official_transcript.asp

Marines / Navy:
https://smart.navy.mil/smart/dod

The following pages feature some examples of what these forms look like:

What Degree Program Is Right for Me? 23

An example of an AARTS transcript evaluation for Army training credit evaluation

Military credits are evaluated by the American Council on Education (ACE). When ACE evaluates a military course, colleges refer to their recommendations for credits to determine what credits may be given for

24 *Military Education Benefits for College*

XXX-XX-   Page 1 of 8

SAILOR/MARINE
AMERICAN COUNCIL ON EDUCATION
REGISTRY TRANSCRIPT

INDIVIDUAL COPY

Transcript Sent To:

Name:
SSN: XXX-XX-
Rank: Staff Sergeant
Status: Active

Military Course Completions

Courses: Recruit Training   ACE Identifier:
                                              MC-2204-0088
                                              Military Course ID:
Date Taken: 25-APR-1994   808

Description:
Upon completion of the course, the male and female graduate recruit will demonstrate knowledge of the code of military conduct, laws of war, history of the U.S. Marine Corps, first aid and field sanitation, and nuclear, biological, and chemical warfare defense; practice military courtesy; demonstrate good personal health, hygiene, and grooming; and successfully meet prescribed marksmanship standards, physical fitness test requirements, skill level in land navigation, and survival swimming requirements. Male recruit training is 464 hours; female recruit training 510-511 hours.

ACE Credit Recommendation:
In the lower-division baccalaureate/associate degree category, 1 semester hour in physical fitness and conditioning, 2 in marksmanship, and 1 in orienteering/outdoor skills (3/92).

Course: Marine Combat   ACE Identifier:
          Infantry School   MC-2204-0105
          Camp Lejeune, NC   Military Course ID:
Date Taken: 27-JUL-1994 To 19-AUG-1994   M92

Description:
Upon completion of the course, the student will possess weapon and infantry skills necessary to function as a

** PRIVACY ACT INFORMATION **   10/28/2009

Example of a smart transcript

that particular military course. See the example on the following page of what that evaluation looks like for a military course.

What Degree Program Is Right for Me? 25

For information on the ACE reviews of your military education, please go to the following website:

www.militaryguides.acenet.edu/showacecourses.asp?aceid=AR-22 01-0253

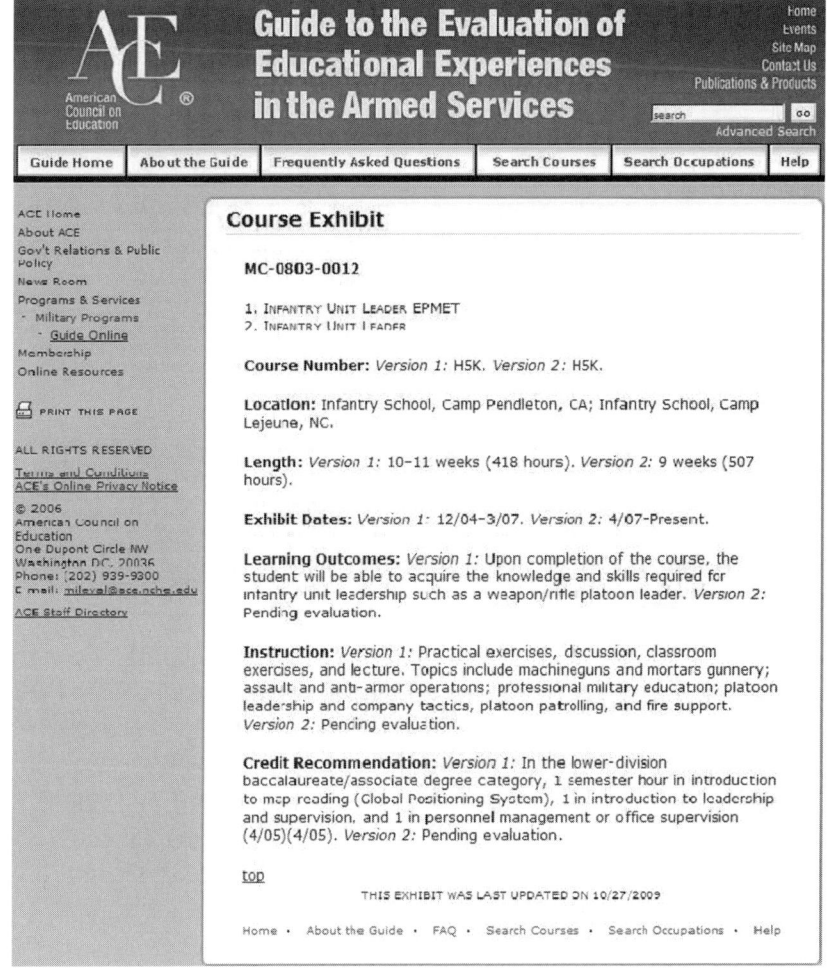

An ACE evaluation of an army course for occupation training.

THE BIG IDEA! *Your military training and schooling may be worth valuable credits that can be transferred to academic institutions. Be sure to speak with your academic advisor to see how many credits can be accepted. Have your transcripts printed and ready for evaluation!*

When obtaining your transcripts, print an unofficial copy off the website yourself and ask for an official copy to be sent to you or the school. Official copies can take a long time to arrive, so ask if your school accepts the unofficial transcripts for an initial evaluation.

CLEP and DANTES

The College Level Examination Program (CLEP) and Defense Activity for Non-Traditional Education Support (DANTES) are two sources of standardized testing that allow the SCS to replace college courses with satisfactory grades on the test. These tests are available in any number of areas and can save you time and money. Courses are available in several areas, including Science, Math, English, Foreign Languages, and History. The reason the CLEP and DANTES tests are helpful are as follows:

- Provide the SCS with an alternative means to taking a class in an area they are already proficient in by demonstrating their knowledge. This is a great option if you know a second language, for example, and may allow you to get credit for something you already know.

- Can be used to avoid taking certain classes, allowing minimal time in the classroom for the SCS and avoid the boredom often associated with taking some lower-level and introductory courses.

- Service branches often allow reimbursement of study materials and the test. Often, education benefits can be used on books to study for the course and to pay for the test once it is taken. Check with your ESO for details.

- Certain tests may be accepted for credits in more than one level of class, particularly in foreign language or English areas.

- Aside from the opportunity for reimbursement, these courses, if accepted as credits at your institution, can save you money since you don't have to take courses at the traditional price at the college you are attending.

With the service branch assisting you in paying for the exam and the option for training to help you pay, these tests may be a valuable resource to you in helping you obtain additional course credits without spending time in a classroom.

LISTEN UP—IMPORTANT POINT!

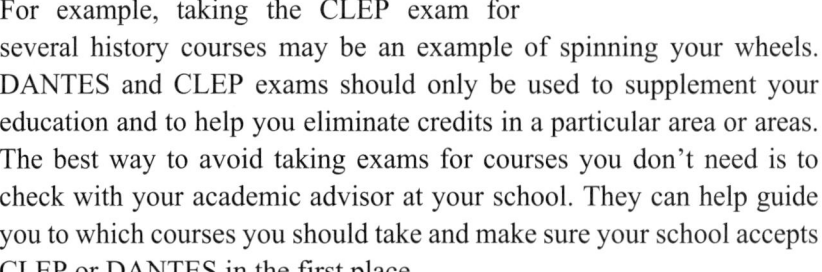

The key is to make sure you are taking courses that will be transferrable to the school to which you are applying. Some schools may have limited curriculums that don't require you to take courses you are taking credits in. For example, taking the CLEP exam for several history courses may be an example of spinning your wheels. DANTES and CLEP exams should only be used to supplement your education and to help you eliminate credits in a particular area or areas. The best way to avoid taking exams for courses you don't need is to check with your academic advisor at your school. They can help guide you to which courses you should take and make sure your school accepts CLEP or DANTES in the first place.

The objective of taking and studying for the exams is to save time and money, so try not to take exams that won't help you in your degree plan, if at all possible. If you take the exam(s) before starting school, this is fine also. However, try to take proficiency exams in areas of basic study, such as English or Science, and not in areas that will fall under the course of study you wish to pursue. The reason this is important is because as you enter into a program that has degree plans in the course of study you wish to pursue, you will find that each school has specific courses designed to meet that curriculum requirement, similar to transferring credits from other programs of study.

Remember also that your objective is not to just get credits in the area you wish to study, but to become <u>knowledgeable</u>. The amount of time you spend taking classes in your area of interest will only enhance your skills when you graduate, and allow you additional opportunities to network with instructors and your fellow classmates.

Educational Support Offices

Educational Support Offices (ESOs) can be a wealth of information to help you when pursuing your education. They are staffed with personnel trained to help you with education paperwork and can provide you with direction and advice when needed. They can also help with questions related (though not limited) to benefits such as tuition assistance and funding education for your dependents.

ESOs should never be making decisions for you; instead, you should use them for sound advice. Remember that your own experiences and needs may be different from those of other SCS they encounter. Don't look to ESOs to help guide you to what you should do, or to research things for you. They are there to guide you to the sources, but you have to be cognizant of your own needs and desires when researching the education steps that are right for you. Don't

THE BIG IDEA! *CLEP and DANTES tests can offer you course credits toward your degree of choice and help evaluate your skills while saving you time and money.*

skip the step of researching on your own to find the best program, school, or career path for you!

A list of ESOs that can help answer questions at active duty bases for all branches of the service throughout the world are listed below:

List of ESOs by Service Branches (subject to change)
Courtesy of MilitaryTA.com

AIR FORCE—WORLDWIDE

Germany: Geilenkirchen, Ramstein AB Kaiserslauten, Ramstein AB, Spangdahlem AB
Guam: Anderson AFB
Iraq: Balad, Kirkuk, Sather AB/BIAP, Tallil
Italy: Aviano AB, Ghedi AB
Japan: Kasenda AB Okinawa, Misawa AB, Yokota AB
Korea: Kunsan AB, Osan AB
Portugal: Lajes Field
Qatar: Al Udeid AB
Turkey: Ankara, Incirlik AB, Izmir AB
United Kingdom: RAF Alconbury Molesworth, RAF Croughton, RAF Fairford, RAF Lakenheath, RAF Menwith Hill, RAF Mildenhall,

AIR FORCE—UNITED STATES

Alaska: Eielson AFB, Elmendorf AFB
Alabama: Maxwell AFB
Arkansas: Little Rock AFB
Arizona: Davis Monthan AFB, Luke AFB
California: Beale AFB, Edwards AFB, Los Angeles AFB, Travis AFB, Vandenberg AFB
Colorado: Buckley AFB, Peterson AFB
Delaware: Dover AFB
District of Columbia: Bolling AFB, Pentagon
Florida: Eglin AFB, Hurlburt Field, Macdill AFB, Patrick AFB, Tyndall AFB
Georgia: Moody AFB, Robins AFB
Hawaii: Hickam AFB
Idaho: Mountain Home AFB
Illinois: Scott AFB
Kansas: McConnell AFB
Louisiana: Barksdale AFB
Massachusetts: Hanscom AFB
Maryland: Andrews AFB, Ft. Mead
Mississippi: Columbus AFB, Keesler AFB
Missouri: Whiteman AFB
Montana: Malmstrom AFB
Nebraska: Offutt AFB
Nevada: Nellis AFB
New Jersey: McGuire AFB
New Mexico: Cannon AFB, Holloman AFB, Kirtland AFB
North Carolina: Pope AFB, Seymour Johnson AFB

North Dakota: Grand Forks AFB, Minot AFB
Ohio: Wright Patterson AFB
Oklahoma: Altus AFB, Tinker AFB, Vance AFB
South Carolina: Charleston AFB, Shaw AFB
South Dakota: Arnold AFB
Tennessee: Arnold AFB
Texas: Brooks City-Base, Dyess AFB, Goodfellow AFB, Greenville, Lackland AFB, Laughlin AFB, Randolph AFB, Sheppard AFB
Utah: Hill AFB
Virginia: Langley AFB
Washington: Fairchild AFB, McChord AFB
Wyoming: F E Warren

ARMY—WORLDWIDE

Afghanistan: Bagram Airfield, Camp Phoenix, FOB Salerna, Kandahar Airfield
Belgium: SHAPE, USAG Brussels
Egypt: North Camp Sinai, South Camp Sinai
Germany: Armstrong Barracks, Cambri Fritsch Kaserne Darmstadt, Dexheim, Giessen Army Depot, HD Smith Barracks Baumholder, Hohenfels, Katterbach AAF, Kleber Army Barracks, Ledward Barracks Schweinfurt, Miesau Depot Kaiserslautern, Panzer Kaserne Stuttgart, Patton Barracks Heidelberg, Pioneer Kaserne Hanau, Rhine Ordinance Barracks, Sullivan Barracks Mannheim, Vilseck, Warner Barracks Bamberg, Wiesbaden Army AF
Honduras:Soto-Canto AB
Iraq: Blackjack-Anaconda
Italy: Camp Darby, Vincenza
Japan: Camp Zama, Torii Station Okinawa
Korea: Camp Carroll,, Camp Casey, Camp Henry, Camp Hovey, Camp Humphreys, Camp Long, Camp Red Cloud, Camp Stanley, Yongsan
Kosovo: Camp Bondsteel, Camp Monteith
Kuwait: Kuwait Installation
Netherlands: Schinnen
Qatar: Camp As Sayliyah

ARMY—UNITED STATES

Alabama: Fort Rucker, Redstone Arsenal
Alaska: Fort Richardson , Fort Wainwright
Arizona: Fort Huachuca, Yuma Proving Ground
California: Fort Irwin, Presidio of Monterey
Colorado: Fort Carson
District of Columbia: Pentagon , Walter Reed
Florida: HQ SOUTHCOM
Georgia: Fort Benning, Fort Gordon, Fort McPherson, Fort Stewart, Hunter Army Airfield
Hawaii: Schofield Barracks, Tripler AMC
Illinois: Rock Island Arsenal
Kansas: Fort Leavenworth, Fort Riley

Kentucky: Fort Leavenworth, Fort Riley
Lousisiana: Fort Polk
Massachusetts: RFTA Devens
Maryland: Aberdeen Proving Grounds, Fort Detrick, Fort Meade
Michigan: Selfridge ANGB
Missouri: Fort Leonard Wood
New Jersey: Fort Dix, Fort Monmouth
New Mexico: White Sands Missle Range
New York: Fort Drum, Fort Hamilton, West Point
North Carolina: Fort Bragg
Oklahoma: Fort Sill
Pennsylvannia: Carlisle Barracks
South Carolina: Fort Jackson
Texas: Fort Bliss, Fort Hood Fort Sam Houston
Utah: Dugway Proving Grounds
Virginia: Fort Belvoir, Fort Eustis, Fort Lee, Fort Monroe, Fort Myer, Fort Story
Washington: Fort Lewis

COAST GUARD—WORLDWIDE

Purerto Rico: CGAS Borinquen

COAST GUARD—UNITED STATES

Alaska: CG SECTOTR Anchorage, CG Seventeenth District, CGAS Sitka, CG Loran Station Port Clarence, CG MSO Valdez, ISC Ketchikan, ISC Kodiak, USCG Hickory, USCG Sycamore
Alabama: CG Sector Mobile, USCG Aviation Training Center
California: CG Sector/Air Station Humboldt Bay, CG Training Center Petaluma, USCGC Blackfin
District of Columbia: U.S. Coast Guard HQ
Florida: CGAS Clearwater, ISC Miami
Hawaii: ISC Honolulu
Iowa: CG Group Upper Mississippi River
Maine: CG Group Upper Mississippi River
Massachusetts: CG Sector NE New England, CGAS Cape Cod, ISC Boston
Michigan: CG Sector Sault St. Marie, CG SFO Grand Haven, CGAS Traverse City
New Jersey: USCG Training Center
New York: CG SFO Mouiches
North Carolina: CGAS Elizabeth City
Ohio: AJC Federal Building, CG MSU Toledo
Oklahoma: USCG Institute
Oregon: CG Group Air Station North Bend, CG Group Astoria, CG Sector Portland
Texas: CG MSU Port Arthur, MSO Houston
Virginia: CG Command Norfolk, CG TISCOM Washington, CG TRACEN Yorktown, ISC Portsmouth
Washington: CGAS Port Angeles, ISC Seattle,
Wisconsin: CG PRO Marinette, CG Sector Lake Michigan

MARINES—WORLDWIDE

Japan: Camp Butler Okinawa, Camp Courtney Okinawa, Camp Foster Okinawa, Camp Fuji Okinawa, Camp Hansen Okinawa, Camp Kinser Okinawa, Camp Schwab Okinawa, MCAS Futenma Okinawa, MCAS Iwakuni

MARINES—UNITED STATES

Arizona: MCAS Yuma
California: Camp Pendleton, MCAS Miramar, MCB Twentynine Palms, MCLB Barstow, MCRD San Diego
Georgia: MCLB Albany
Hawaii: Kaneohe Bay and Camp HM Smith
Massachusetts: RFT Area Fort Devens
North Carolina: Camp Lejeune, MCAS Cherry Point, MCAS NR Jacksonville
South Carolina: MCAS Beaufort, MCRD Parris Island
Virginia: Henderson Hall, MCB Quantico

NAVY—WORLDWIDE

Bahrain: NSA Bahrain
Cuba: Guantanamo Bay
Diego Garcia: NSF Diego Garcia
Greece: NSA Souda Bay
Guam: COMNAVMARINAS
Italy: NAS Sigonella, NSA Naples
Japan: CFA Kadena, CFA Sasebo, CFA Yokosuka, Misawa AB, NAF Atsugi
Spain: Naval Station Rota

NAVY—UNITED STATES

California: NAS Lemoore, NAVMEDCEN San Diego, Naval Base Coronado, Naval Base Point Loma, Naval Base San Diego, Naval Brig Miramar, NAWS China Lake, NBVC Point Mugu, NBVC Port Hueneme
Connectiut: Submarine Base Groton
District of Columbia: Naval District Washington
Florida: NAS Jacksonville, NAS Key West, NAS Saufley Field, NAVSTA Mayport
Georgia: Submarine Base Kings Bay
Hawaii: Naval Station Pearl Harbor
Illinois: Naval Station Great Lakes
Louisiana: NSA New Orleans
Maine: NAS Brunswick
Maryland: NAS Patuxent River, NNMC Bethesda
Mississippi: NAS Meridian, Naval Construction BN CNTR Gulfport
Nevada: NAS Fallon
New Jersey: Naval Air Engineering Station
New York: NPTU Ballston SPA
Oklahoma: Tinker AFB
Rhode Island: NAVSTA Newport
South Carolina: Naval Brig Charleston, Naval Weapons Station Charlesoton
Tennessee: NSA Millington

Texas: NAS Corpus Christi, NAS JRB Fort Worth, NAS Kingsville, Naval Station Ingleside

Virginia: NAB Little Creek, NAS Oceana, NAS Oceana Dam Neck Annex NAVPHIBASE Little Creek, NAVSTA Norfolk, Naval Brig Norfolk, NMC Portsmouth

Washington: NAS Whidbey Island, Naval Base Kitsap, Naval Base Kitsap at Bangor, Naval Station Everett

CHAPTER 4

How Do I Select a School?

"Intelligence plus character—that is the goal of real education."
— Dr. Martin Luther King Jr.

Selecting a School: Start Here!

Researching colleges can be a major undertaking because there is more to it than just calling up an Admissions Counselor and saying, "Sign me up!" To assist you in your investigation and research, we have provided you with a tool in the form of a series of questions you should ask of an Admissions Counselor or, through your online research, find on a college's website.

The list of 20 questions have been developed with you, the SCS, in mind because they are the things that should be the most important to you. You will find the list below. We have also provided an additional copy in Appendix 2 that you can tear out, copy, and make notes on for each school you research. Also in Appendix 2, we have provided you with a decision matrix to assist you with making your final decision.

INSTRUCTIONS: Reach each question carefully. Place either a +1 (plus one) in the "Yes" column, or a -1 (minus one) in the "No" column. For the six questions in bold (Nos. 1, 3, 6, 8, 19, and 20), place either a + 3 (plus three) or a –3 (minus three) because these questions should be given more weight.

SCHOOL		YES	NO
Q-1	**Is the school a member of SOC?**		
Q-2	Is the school Nationally Accredited?		
Q-3	**Is the school Regionally Accredited?**		
Q-4	Is the school certified to receive GI Bill Benefits?		
Q-5	Is the school a Yellow Ribbon participating school?		
Q-6	**Does the school offer both traditional classes and online classes?**		
Q-7	If you attend as a traditional student, can you transfer to an online program without penalty?		

Q-8	Can you have your military training and experience evaluated for college credits before enrolling as a student?		
Q-9	Does the college offer a special tuition program for military students?		
Q-10	Does the college offer a special tuition program for veterans?		
Q-11	Does the college offer a special tuition program for military dependents?		
Q-12	Is there an application fee for military members, veterans, or military dependants?		
Q-13	Can you stay enrolled if you miss more than one term due to a military related requirement?		
Q-14	Does the school provide a waiver for the SCS on fees?		
Q-15	Does the school have experience in dealing with SCS students?		
Q-16	Does the school have a Veterans Affairs or similar office?		
Q-17	Does the school have a Career Services office that has experience in working with veterans and translating military training and experience into a viable resume?		
Q-18	Once you are ready to apply, can you do so in person and complete all required paperwork and, if required, placement testing during a scheduled campus visit?		
Q-19	If you receive Tuition Assistance as a reimbursement, can you pay for your tuition once you receive your TA instead of paying up front?		

Q-20	**If you are ordered to active duty, does the school have a flexible withdraw policy for military students?**

YOUR PERSONAL NOTES

Accreditation

The first place to begin in your inquiry of finding a school is to understand the difference between national accreditation and regional accreditation. Accreditation is defined by the U.S. Department of Education as "a voluntary, non-governmental process in which an institution and its programs are evaluated against standards for measuring quality." Why is this important? The most obvious reason is that if the college or university is not accredited, the degree, certificate, or credential that you earn (whether you use your own money, use your service provided tuition assistance program, or use your GI Bill benefit), is not worth the paper it is written on. Therefore, accreditation is very important.

As a minimum, the school that you select to earn your degree from or even just to take a few courses with, should at least be nationally accredited by the U.S. Department of Education (USDE). A college that is nationally accredited will be accredited by any one of dozens of national accrediting organizations. These organizations are often for-profit schools, and many offer programs that are less academic in nature and more vocational or technical-oriented than traditional universities, and some only offer certificates rather than degrees.

Below are some of the more popular examples of national accrediting institutions:

- Distance Education and Training Council

- Accrediting Council for Independent Colleges and Schools

- Accrediting Commission of Career Schools and Colleges of Technology

- Accrediting Council for Continuing Education and Training

LISTEN UP—IMPORTANT POINT!

One of the biggest misconceptions we see in admissions from incoming students is the belief that a national accreditation is a stronger accreditation than a regional one. This is often not the case. In fact, because of their close proximity to the campuses of their institutions they accredit, the regional accrediting institutions hold very high academic standards, frequently auditing their records to make sure the schools are performing at the highest standard and offering a quality education. Because this level of accountability is commonplace for these institutions, schools will often accept similar credits from another regionally accredited school if they will fit into their degree plan and their curriculum.

However, some employers will only acknowledge degrees from a regionally accredited college or university. Why the difference? It all has to do with standards. Basically, a college or university receives national accreditation from the USDE and the Council of Higher Education Accreditation (CHEA) by following and adhering to the national standards required for accreditation. Those colleges and universities that are also regionally accredited voluntarily participate in a further, more stringent, level of accreditation by one of the seven regional accreditation bodies:

- Middle States Association of Colleges and Schools Middle States Commission on Higher Education (MSCHE);

- New England Association of Schools and Colleges Commission on Institutions of Higher Education (NEASC-CIHE);

- North Central Association of Colleges and Schools The Higher Learning Commission (NCA-HCL);

- Northwest Commission on Colleges and Universities (NWCCU);

- Southern Association of Colleges and Schools Commission on Colleges (SACS);

- Western Association of Schools and Colleges Accrediting Commission for Community and Junior Colleges (WASC-ACCJC); and

- Western Association of Schools and Colleges Accrediting Commission for Senior Colleges and Universities (WASC-ACSCU).

The Council for Higher Education Accreditation maintains a detailed directory and information on each of the accrediting organizations. "The accrediting organizations identified in this directory are recognized by the Council for Higher Education Accreditation (CHEA). Recognition by CHEA affirms that the standards and processes of the accrediting organization are consistent with the academic quality, improvement and accountability expectations that CHEA has established, including the eligibility standard that the majority of institutions or programs each accredits are degree-granting."

Each of these accrediting commissions grants accreditation to participating colleges and universities based on a set of standards that are established by each accrediting commission. Colleges and universities that are regionally accredited by these commissions maintain their accreditation through periodic reviews of their degree programs and curriculum, administration policies and procedures, and academic policies and procedures.

Within the academic world, accreditation is not taken lightly, and you should not take it lightly either when selecting a college or university from which you wish to earn your degree. We recommend that the school that you select in earning your degree be part of one of the above accrediting bodies.

LISTEN UP—IMPORTANT POINT!

Accreditation also plays into the transferability of college credits earned with one institution that are accepted by another. As a general rule of thumb, any college credits earned from a regionally accredited college or university will be accepted by any other regionally or nationally accredited college or university. However, the converse is not always true. College credits earned from a nationally accredited college or university *may* or *may not* be accepted by a regionally accredited college or university. Why? The reason again is accreditation standards. Remember, a regionally accredited college or university has to go through an additional level of standards before being accredited. As such, not all nationally accredited credits will be accepted by regionally accredited schools. As such, their credits may not be accepted for transfer. Be careful about this—particularly if you are thinking about transferring schools at a later time, or going for an advanced degree down the road.

A Cautionary Tale: Watch out for Diploma and Degree Mills

A brief caution about diploma and degree mills is in order. "Diploma Mills" are institutions that offer fake degrees from real colleges. "Degree Mills" are institutions that offer real degrees from fake colleges.

There are several characteristics to look out for when looking for diploma or degree mills:

- Academic credits or degrees given for "life experience";

- No faculty members with advanced degrees;

- Charges are given for entire degrees rather than per course;

- No accreditation, or accreditation by a false institution;

- Minimal requirements for course accountability;

- Institution name sounds like another accredited institution.

These are telltale signs of diploma and degree mills that <u>should</u> send up an immediate red flag in your search. If you have a hunch that a school you are considering is a diploma or degree mill, check their accreditation status to be certain. Beware of these "schools" at all cost. If you have any doubt, don't enroll. Remember that your benefits should not be wasted on a piece of paper. The journey to a college degree or certificate is as important as the destination, which is why employers and reputable universities will not accept such degrees. Nothing in your military career ever came easy, and if there's a way to buy yourself a degree or certificate, then that should give you a reason to think something isn't right.

LISTEN UP—IMPORTANT POINT!

You cannot buy a college degree. Accredited colleges and universities all have minimum residency requirements as imposed by their accrediting body. The minimum residency requirements are the minimum number of credits that the student must take with the college or university in order for the college or university to confer a degree diploma. This type of degree is not worth the paper it is printed on. If you get one of these and use it for promotion purposes or in any other way, you may find yourself out of the military under less than honorable conditions.

Another entity to be wary of is the credit bank. A credit bank is an agency, an accredited college or university or, more often, it will be an extension of an accredited college or university that maintains a repository of data on a multitude of military and civilian training programs and occupations and their recommended ACE college credits.

How does a credit bank work? You send them copies of your military transcripts, certifications, efficiency reports, etc., along with a check. In return, they send you a "college transcript." The transcript is just a listing of college credits based on your military training and experience and is NOT an academic degree program. Many colleges and universities do not accept credit bank transcripts for the vetting of college credits; nor do employers. If you pay for the services of a credit bank, you are paying for something that will not assist you at all in applying for a job or getting ahead academically. Save your money and your dignity.

THE BIG IDEA! *The more you know about the accreditation and academic standing of the schools you are considering, the more certain you will be that supervisors, potential employers and other schools will hold your certificate or degree—and yourself—in high regard!*

Servicemembers Bill of Rights

The second thing that you need to investigate when searching for a school is to find out if it is a member of SOC—the Servicemembers Opportunity Colleges network. The SOC network is a consortium of member colleges and universities that agree to adhere to standard practices and policies as they relate to servicing military students. As such, SOC has established a "Military Student Bill of Rights." In 2006, the president of SOC asked for a complete review of the recruiting, marketing, and student services practices among SOC colleges and universities. The result was the requirement for all member colleges and universities to adhere to the "Military Student Bill of Rights."

All military students have the basic right to satisfactory practices by colleges and universities with regard to recruiting, admissions, and student services. As a military student you have the right to expect the following from any of the SOC member colleges or universities:

- Accurate information about the school's programs, requirements, accreditation, and its potential impact on course transferability;

- Access to basic college/university information and fees without disclosure of personal information;

- Educational planning and career guidance without high-pressure registration and enrollment efforts from institutions;

- A clear and complete explanation of course/program enrollment procedures and all resulting financial obligations;

- The ability to explore, without coercion, all financial aid options before signing up for student loans or other financial assistance;

- Accurate scholarship information, free of misleading "scholarship" offers based on military tuition assistance;

- Appropriate academic screening and course placement based on student readiness;

- Appropriate, accessible academic and student support services;

- Clearly defined institutional "add/drop" and withdrawal policies and procedures including information about the impact of military duties (i.e mobilization, activation, TDY assignments, etc.) on their academic standing and financial responsibilities;

- Clearly defined grievance/appeals process.

SOC member colleges and universities agree to adhere and support these standards and the Military Student Bill of Rights. Unfortunately, though, not all SOC schools do. This is not intended to slight or cast any shadows on any SOC member school. It is to inform you, the military student, of your rights and what you should expect as a student from a SOC member school. Colleges and universities that have dedicated military student support services and staff are generally able to better adhere and support the Military Student Bill of Rights.

Another major consideration for you, the military service connected student, is how does the school view or accept military training and experience for college credit. Again, if the college is a SOC member school, there are standard practices that all colleges and universities agree to follow. One of them is to accept the college credit recommendations of the American Council on Education (ACE) recommendations. One of ACE's main purposes is to evaluate military training and experience and provide its member schools with recommendations on the equivalent college level credits and in what discipline the credits should be applied. Notice that they are <u>recommendations</u>. The general understanding and agreement is that colleges and universities will award college credits for military training and experience based on the ACE recommendations. However, each college and university is within its rights <u>not</u> to accept the ACE recommendation.

LISTEN UP—IMPORTANT POINT!

Though a school may accept the recommendation of ACE, they may limit the amount of credits that can be transferred into a particular degree program for your military training and experiences. For example, you are a Sergeant First Class in the Army and you have completed all of your military educational requirements and have a number of military occupational skills. Your AARTS transcript shows that you have in excess of 90 college credits based on the recommendations of ACE. However, the school that you are applying to will only accept 12 "life learning credits" from any source. Another example, based on the previous situation: the college informs you that they will award all 90 credits to you. You think this is fantastic, and you will be able to complete your degree in no time. You enroll with the school only to find out that only 24 credits were actually accepted into your degree plan and that the other credits are "non-degree requirement credits." Clearly, either case is frustrating to you, the military student.

In any case, you should ask the schools you are considering *if and how they accept military training and experience for college credits.* Make sure to ask how many credits in total will they accept from the military and how are they articulated into your specific degree program.

Now, a word of warning regarding college credits for military training and experience:

Do not, under any circumstance, send money to a college or university to confer upon you a degree based solely on your military training or experience!

Military-Friendly Schools

There are a lot of factors to consider during your search in determining the right school for you. In this section, we provide you with some critical elements to consider when researching schools. The elements presented are by no means all-inclusive, and they are not meant to be the only ones you consider. Based upon our experience, however, these elements are the most important when trying to make the decision of where to attend college as a service-connected student.

During your research into schools, you will undoubtedly come across the phrase "Military Friendly School." You will find this phrase in college literature, advertisements, and on college websites. In the majority of cases, this is a term used by the college as a marketing attempt to attract unknowing members of the military or veterans to their school. Remember, you are a potential customer to a college and colleges expend millions of dollars every year to make the best pitch possible to get you to come to their school. If you see the phrase "Military Friendly," tread cautiously and remember to ask the right questions that we provided you.

What really determines if a school should be classified as "Military Friendly"? There is no formal evaluation process of colleges by an external agency to evaluate colleges and determine their degree of military friendliness. However, there are a few agencies that do provide a listing of "Military Friendly Schools." *Military Advanced Education (MAE)* is a periodical that focuses on the education of our nation's military. *MAE* links the professional military education network of Education Support Officer (ESO) and support offices and college

48   *Military Education Benefits for College*

THE BIG IDEA! *Military-friendly schools are fully prepared to meet the needs of military students, from understanding the paperwork for payment methods to helping the SCS get military credits evaluated. If researched correctly, such institutions can help meet the needs of the SCS and help them achieve their education goals.*

educators in a forum in which they can share information, describe best practices, and collaborate on educating today's military members. The *MAE* publishes an annual list of "military friendly schools" that can provide you a starting point for your research into finding the right school for you.

Another very useful tool you can use is the Military One Source website at www.militaryonesource.com. This website will provide you with information on a number of subjects including education (searching for schools), funding education, and a host of other educational-related topics. However, one thing to remember is that, as with any website, businesses and colleges pay to be listed on websites and just because you find colleges listed on this or any other website which tailors its message to the military does not mean that the college is a truly "Military Friendly" college.

Transcript Information

Another source for finding out the amount of college credit that your military training/experience is worth is the VMET website: www.dmdc.osd.mil/appj/vmet/logindisplay.do. VMET stands for the Verification of Military and Training. The site is hosted by the Department of Defense and requires you to verify your current or previous military service. The information contained within VMET comes from a number of official sources and official personnel records. If you find that there are items missing, you should contact your personnel office if you are still serving in the military or submit a DD Form 149, Application for Correction of Military Records. The form allows you to provide the information needed and where to send the information that requires correction. Please realize that it will take several months for your official records to be updated. Also, VMET is not an official or unofficial transcript. It merely provides you with an indication of how many college credits your military training and experience is worth, and you can use this information when working with colleges on your transfer credits.

The Importance of Support From Your University

In selecting a college to attend, one of the considerations that you should take into account in your decision making is what student resources the school provides to you, the service connected student. Why is this important? As a service connected student you may have been out of the educational mainstream for a while and you need to know that colleges offer more than just classes in a traditional classroom or online setting. Think of your university staff similar to your military leadership. Like their military counterparts in your chain of command and support channels, the support that is provided to you from the offices of a college or university is there to ensure your mission accomplishment and to provide you with the help and the tools to be successful.

Here are some important ones to consider:

- Academic Advising

- Career Services

- Library Services and Research Assistance

- Tutoring Services

- Financial Aid Services

- Veteran's Affairs and Assistance

LISTEN UP—IMPORTANT POINT!

Having an Academic Advisor is an important support person to the success of any student, but for the SCS it is <u>critically</u> important. During your investigation of schools, you should inquire as to what kind of academic advisement is available to you, the SCS. An important question to ask up front is whether or not you will have your own dedicated academic advisor or will there be an advisement pool that your issues or questions are sent to in which to resolve. Having your own academic advisor is much more valuable to you than a pool of advisors who may not offer a high degree of personalized attention. You will form a professional academic relationship with your advisor, and he or she will be better able to assist you as you work through your degree if he has worked with you from the time you started school. Your academic advisor will be able to assist you with determining your academic load per term, and course selection for the term. You academic advisor will also assist you when it comes time to graduate by helping with your final degree audit and your application for graduation.

Also, you should determine if academic advisors understand the challenges that face the SCS, including the possibility of a sudden deployment. Having a full understanding of the challenges that face the military student allows an advisor to better support the military student from term to term. In some respects an academic advisor is like your squad leader. He can help guide you in the direction you want to go, is usually the first one to handle your administrative issues, and serves as your first step in the academic chain of command to voice any questions or concerns.

Career Services is one of the more important support services for college students. Career Services provide students with support in resume writing, employment networking opportunities, and job placement. For the SCS, a college with a Career Services staff that understands the military—and thus how to translate military training and experience into relevant terms and put them into a viable resume—is a major benefit. Your service to the military has provided you with extensive training, experience, and most of all, a great deal of responsibility. Translating your training and experience into a resume is not an easy task and requires someone who has been trained in how to do it. The Career Services staff at the college that you select should have the training and experience necessary to best assist you in developing a resume that captures your valuable experience and training in terms that civilian employers can understand and relate to.

If you are a veteran or the dependent of a veteran, the college that you select should have an office of Veterans Affairs (or a similar office) that you can go to if you have issues or need assistance with processing benefits. This office can also connect you with the right agency within the VA to assist you with other veteran-related issues. Many states have regional VA offices, but these may be many miles away from where you are going to school. Having a Veterans Affairs office on your college campus will allow you to get the support that you need without having to travel or inquire elsewhere. If you are an online student-veteran, you should still be able to contact the Veteran's Affairs Office and receive assistance and support.

Changing Schools

We can all empathize with the lifestyle of a busy student. Being a SCS often means that your lifestyle as a student is even further compromised. A student who is in the military and is transferred to another duty station or is called away on a deployment often has his education plans (at the very least) put on hold, and at worst transferred to another institution down the road.

Changing schools is something that often happens for military students. In our admissions jobs, we see countless students who are transferring in credits—sometimes from several different schools! While

THE BIG IDEA! Your potential school(s) should strive to offer each student the individual attention he or she deserves, with a specific advisor responsible for your academic well being, and a host of other support staff to make the transition between military life and the classroom as painless as possible, and to make sure your experience is enriching and rewarding.

this is certainly understandable and more often times than not the norm, this is something that doesn't have to be. At times, military students make quick decisions with their education because it's something they are used to doing with their military occupations. Sometimes, due to uncertainty about what classes are right for them, they may decide not to take courses in any particular area to get acclimated to college.

We're not saying that's a problem. What we are saying is be careful that you are spending both your time in your school and your education benefits wisely. *Think before jumping in and taking a course, and be sure you have consulted with an academic advisor before simply registering for your class.* You may see it as a nuisance to have to speak with a representative from the school, and with online registrations, universities make it easier than ever to just sign up for classes. But it will be worth your time to make sure you choose the right courses to take to make sure you maximize your education benefits.

Let's say you're a relatively young military person or a veteran who's just getting back to school. In both cases, the SCS is uncertain of what classes to take, and uncertain of where to attend school. If this is the case, we suggest that you take core courses primarily that will transfer readily into other universities. These courses can include:

- *Basic English* (English Composition, English Composition and Literature);

- *Math* (College Algebra, College Calculus, Statistics);

- *Science* (Biology, Physics, Chemistry);

- *Social Science* (Psychology, Sociology, Government, Political Science);

- *Humanities* (History, Art, Music, Language, Communications);

- *General Education Electives* (Typically include any courses taken for credit that do not fit into your particular degree plan. These can be transferred credits from another institution or credits from your military experience.)

LISTEN UP—IMPORTANT POINT!

A key to remember is not to take too many courses in one particular area. Different colleges have different stipulations for how many of each requirement is allowed in. For example, a liberal arts program will have more flexibility for you to take humanities courses, but a professional degree program will not, and will usually put these courses into your general electives credits until that area is maxed out. If you have military service on your transcript, your electives will fill up very quickly!

As we just pointed out about electives, those of you who were in the military must keep in mind that you have a record of military courses you have already taken that are eligible for college credits. Most advisors will be able to analyze your military training and schooling for credits, so have your appropriate service-related documentation ready. (Refer to the previous section for the forms indigenous to each branch.) Your DD-214 should be available, as it may be needed to confirm your eligibility for certain programs. In addition, older veterans who haven't been in the service for 20 or more years may need their DD-214 for verification of training, as records of a certain age are not available on these websites.

Also, if you are certain of what program you want to pursue, don't look at the short term. Find out an estimation of how long the program will take, being careful to look at the pace you want to go (full-time or part-time). Analyze your lifestyle throughout what you believe the duration of the program would be. Fully consider your military, employment, and family plans before committing to a program at a school and before giving yourself a time frame to complete your goals.

Keep in mind you may need or want to take time off for military deployments, work, family, or for a little relaxation. Make sure you known the rules and matriculation (registration) requirements at each school. Some require you to re-start the admissions process after a certain amount of time without taking classes (usually more than one year), and in some instances you may have to re-matriculate (re-register) again. Delaying the process for any time more than a few years could mean that the curriculum has changed during that time. Schools often reevaluate programs to determine changes in curricula. This is not to punish students who stopped their education for this reason or that reason, but rather as a response to the rapidly changing professional fields for which they are preparing students. Classes taken in computer and technology fields are changed with great frequency as changes in the field happen extremely rapidly. The same holds true for classes in business and marketing as new methods and responses to consumer demands are quickly met in the classroom. Not only will the curriculum and requirements for programs change frequently, but you may also find that classes that you have already taken may no longer be part of your degree program! However, once you obtain your degree or certificate, no amount of changes to the curriculum or the requirements can reverse the documentation you hold in your hand to supervisors and potential employers—all the more reason to make certain you are committed to seeing your academic goals be achieved in a timely manner!

LISTEN UP—IMPORTANT POINT!

As mentioned before, you may find yourself needing to transfer to another school for any number of reasons, but keep in mind that the time you took to decide on your school and to wind your way through the admissions process was invaluable for planning your education. Picking up and moving to another school (which is frequently due to indecision or lifestyle changes) does little to help you reach your goals. In fact, it often undermines them. While most schools transfer credits for similar courses, programs between two schools are never identical, and you can guarantee that even a transfer to two state schools within the same state under the same academic leadership can still result in a swing of about 10 or so credits against you. That's nearly a full semester's worth of work wasted.

Now, imagine doing that several times during your military career and how much class time you have potentially wasted if you change programs frequently. This is what makes your decision of choosing your school a critical step that should not be taken lightly.

Changing Degree Programs

The hectic and unstable lifestyles of many SCS are not conducive to the traditional college classroom setting. As mentioned previously, SCS who serve can change military occupations and locations many times throughout their military careers. Their lifestyles change, as do their priorities. Maybe starting a family, taking on a job with increased responsibilities, or a deployment push their educational goals to the back burner for awhile.

With all of these changes, attending school with a focused degree plan can be difficult. This is certainly understandable. However, like changing schools, it is something you should avoid whenever possible. It is important to your career, your family, and your livelihood to be able to pick a degree plan and university and, as much as possible, stick with it.

Example: At our school (Post University), we encounter a large number of SCS who served a long time in the military and are looking to, at long last, finish their college degrees. When we ask to see their transcripts from previous schools, they often provide as many as three to five transcripts containing several credits—many of which are in different degree areas. Some of them have the credits equivalent to more than a bachelor's degree! But the courses were taken at different schools with varying or unfocused curriculum and, because they aren't in any specific degree area, many of the credits are not transferable to a more focused degree program. Civilian students call college jumpers likes this "career students." What's more, these transcripts often cost money and can take weeks or even months to arrive depending on the time of year and the guidelines for each institution set by the registrar or records office.

This is the type of habit that, if broken early or avoided altogether, will reap you the rewards of a college degree at a much faster pace. Though you may be awarded administrative promotion points for college credits, many branches of the service are moving away from that practice and only award promotion points for attaining a college degree.

Additionally, changing degrees may also make some credits that you obtained previously non-transferable. Changing degree plans (particularly from areas of liberal arts to general studies as many SCS do when finally realizing the careers they want) can mean that a large number of your credits that fit into one degree plan may not fit into another. As mentioned previously, this can also happen when transferring credits to other schools because different schools have different courses making up their curriculum. Choosing a degree is just as important as choosing the school itself.

It is also important to commit not just to going to school, but choosing a school and a degree plan that you are going to have the opportunity and the motivation to see through to the end. This should always be considered when starting school because it will save you time and, for those of you using your GI Bill, student loans, or savings to fund some or all of your education, it will save you money. Think of your educational journey as a missile, and your goals as the target. Failure to aim that missile in the right direction will mean having to fire more missiles, which in turn costs more money. The missiles you already fired in the wrong direction are wasted and, like classes that can't be transferred into other degree programs, are now useless. Efficiently choosing classes and degree plans is the best way to maximize your benefits.

THE BIG IDEA! *Changing schools may be an unavoidable part of military life. However, the more planning you do at the front end of your education—and the more committed you are to seeing those goals through—the greater chance you have of achieving your goals and academic success without changing schools!*

What Are Your Options?

You've heard a lot about the schools out there. There's no shortage of pamphlets at your Education Support Office or Internet websites advertising colleges—in particular, military-friendly institutions. It's in their best interest to garner your attention because the veteran student population, in particular those who are still active members of the military, come with numerous payment options such as tuition assistance and the GI Bill that enable schools to get paid from an extremely reliable source.

Your educational goals and desire to see them spent for wisely compels you to choose which school is right for you, and part of that process involves analyzing the variety of schools that exist. For example:

- *Technical/Trade Schools*: These are excellent choices for technical career choices (electrician, mechanic, etc.). Offer certifications for several non-administrative careers from automotive repair to plumbing. May be difficult to transfer academic credits to other institutions depending on accreditation. Check to see if the technical or trade school that you are investigating is approved to accept GI Bill Benefits and can also offer financial aid.

- *Community and Junior Colleges*: Offer two-year degrees and certificates in a variety of areas, often at a fraction of the cost of private schools or public four-year colleges. Many states offer tuition waivers for veterans at community colleges, which further enhances their options. A cost-effective way to start your education.

- *State Colleges and Universities*: Typically offer a full-range of undergraduate and graduate degrees. The flagship state institutions and other schools in larger states also offer world-class doctorate programs, law, and medical schools. Often cost less than private schools due to state funding and many states offer veterans and active military tuition waivers at these schools.

- *Private Schools*: Private schools offering full range of undergraduate and graduate courses, many offering doctorate, law, and medical programs. Majority of funding provided by higher tuition and endowments provided by alumni.

At the onset, the type of program—and not the cost of the program—should be the key determining factor for which schools you consider. If you plan wisely, the military benefits you have earned as an SCS can afford you the option to go to many schools out of reach of other students. Also, the format of program you choose should reflect the flexibility of your schedule and your goals for degree completion.

Here are some examples:

- *Traditional Programs*: Attending school with traditional classes, typically offered during the day in blocks of anywhere from 1-3 hours.

- *Night/Weekend Programs*: Offered by several institutions to reflect the number of professional students looking to return to school. Often offering advanced or certificate programs at an accelerated pace.

- *Low Residency Programs*: An increasingly offered feature by schools as a hybrid of their traditional classroom settings with online or distance learning courses. Often include a combination of reduced classroom time in the form of shortened semesters or concentrated lectures with instructors and other students in combination with online submissions or pre-arranged course material between student and the instructor.

- *Online Programs*: Allow the student the opportunity to participate in classes in an online format where instructors and fellow students communicate online and post assignments via threaded discussion boards. May also feature opportunity to take classes on campus for those close by.

While each of these programs offer distinct advantages, each also has its shortcomings. The traditional classroom environment is still the tried and true version of the college experience we've become accustomed to, and one that still offers the most popular choice for education. Non-traditional distance learning and online programs, however, are catching on fast. In their infancy they were associated with correspondence course institutions and diploma mills that promised certifications and degrees for fast cash. That image is rapidly fading. With the recognition that it's getting tougher and tougher for working professionals to sit in a traditional classroom two or three times per week, reputable universities and colleges have created their own distance and online education programs with similar, if not identical, course requirements and curricula to their own traditional programs.

LISTEN UP—IMPORTANT POINT!

Considering the often tumultuous schedules and lifestyles of SCS still in the military, distance and online programs now offer the most viable options for military personnel and working veterans.

While the initial word about diploma and degree mills hurt the reputation of many of these programs, this stigma has been quieted by the emergence of quality programs. Several reputable institutions are now offering alternatives to a traditional classroom degree plan, and even top state universities and Ivy League institutions associated with traditional classrooms have recently joined the foray of offering online and distance courses and, in some cases, entire programs dedicated to bringing quality education alternatives to adult learners.

If you are in a military status with frequent change in duty stations, occupational challenges, or possibility for deployment, or are involved in a career or family obligations that don't allow you the opportunity to attend school two to three times a week in a traditional campus, the online or low residency requirement programs may be a great alternative to you to ensure you are able to achieve your educational goals without putting them off any further.

Of course, as with any other schools, be sure to check the academic accreditation of these programs carefully.

* * *

You have now completed your initial research on colleges and college programs; you have determined the type of degree program that you want; and you have found several schools that offer your chosen degree program. It is now time to move on to the next step: the College Admissions Process.

Use the tools in Appendix 2 to assist you in your research and to make your decision.

THE BIG IDEA! *Inventory on your needs as a SCS and as a person with military, career, and family responsibilities will lead you to properly determine the type of program that best serves your needs. The options out there are virtually limitless for you to find a program just right for you to get started. Do your research carefully and you will achieve your academic goals before you know it!*

CHAPTER 5

The College Admissions Process

"A man who has never gone to school may steal from a freight car; but if he has a university education, he may steal the whole railroad."

— Theodore Roosevelt

College Admissions: The Process

In general, all schools follow the same basic admissions process. In any event, you should ask the admissions counselor about what the actual process is, and how long it will take before you are notified of your acceptance. The process may be different if you plan on earning your degree as a "resident" student—meaning you will be taking your classes in a traditional classroom—or if you will be pursuing your degree in a distance learning or online format.

The general process is outlined below:

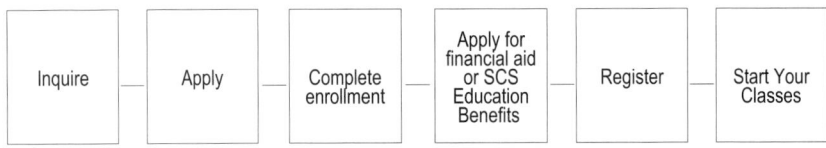

Whether you will be a first-time college student, or you will be transferring to or from another college, the process is basically the same. In the next chapter, we will go into detail on selecting the right school for you, which will allow you to narrow your search down to a select three to five schools in which you will want to inquire further.

Most schools allow you to undergo the admissions process in person; this is typically done on campus with an admissions specialist. Some traditional programs may require it. In some cases, you can contact them via a toll-free number; on some websites they may even give you the name of the representative and an email address. In some cases, you may have requested information on a particular website relating to education benefits that triggers an admissions representative to contact you. Some schools will have an admissions counselor speak to you and then have you speak to a VA representative or a military liaison for the school who will assist you with your needs as an SCS. Other schools will have a military enrollment coordinator who assists you with all facets of the admissions process to include helping you with tuition assistance or obtaining your GI Bill benefits.

LISTEN UP—IMPORTANT POINT!

Either way, it is extremely critical that as soon as contact is initiated between yourself and the school, you let them know immediately that you are a SCS. The best way to do this is to simply announce to them that you are an active military member, veteran, or dependent before the conversation changes to degree plans, cost, etc. The sooner you do this in the admissions process, the easier it will be for the school to make sure the right person is talking to you and that they offer you exactly what you deserve as an SCS.

This is important for three reasons: (1) If you wait too long, you could already make a payment to the school before realizing that you were eligible for a discount or to have payment deferred. With some schools, the refunding process can take some time, so it's important to not even let it get that far. (2) You may be denying yourself potential credits if your institution or degree plan will let military credits transfer in. (3) Your admissions counselor, VA representative, or liaison may be able to assist you with paperwork and make your process much smoother. Let them know about your status right away!

Inquire

Once you have narrowed your search down to a select few schools, you will want to inquire with each of them to find out more about the programs they offer and what special programs, scholarships, and discounts they may offer you, the SCS. Keep one thing in mind during your inquiry phase: you are the customer! Yes, you are a customer and you are in the "market" for a college education. Colleges and universities invest a great deal of money in marketing their programs and drawing you to their websites. As a customer, make sure that you get the opportunity to speak to an admissions or enrollment representative who you can ask specific questions to and—hopefully—get specific answers from. However, do not be hasty in completing an online inquiry form to request information. You can gain a great deal of information about the school simply by browsing their website. You should only complete an online inquiry form when you are ready and have researched the school fully.

When you do inquire with a school, you should expect to receive both electronic and hard copy marketing and information materials that will outline your next steps to follow with that particular school. Many schools have deadlines for the submission of key documents and information. If you do not meet those deadlines, it could delay your admissions process.

When you complete an online inquiry form, make sure the information you enter is correct: spelling is important and complete all fields. Note: If you are on the internet browsing for general information about college, and you click on what is called an "aggregator" site like e-learners, be prepared to receive a large number of phone calls and emails from every school that uses that particular aggregator to generate their leads. Remember, higher education is a business, and you are a potential customer.

During your inquiry of a particular school, here are a few things that you should look for on their website or ask of the enrollment representative:

- Is there a separate section of the website devoted to military students?

- Does the college offer special tuition rates for members of the military, veterans/retirees, and dependents?

- Does the college offer any other special programs, i.e., free books, etc., for members of the military, veterans/retirees, and dependents?

- If applying to an online school, is the college just an online school, or is it a "traditional brick and mortar school" with an online program?

- Is there an application fee or any other fees?

- What is the school's accreditation?

- Is the college a member of SOC—Servicemembers Opportunity Colleges network?

- Is the college eligible to receive GI Bill Educational Benefits to pay for college costs?

- Does the college have an office or person who handles GI Bill questions and issues?

- What are the minimum residency requirements in order to earn a degree from the college?

- Does the college provide college credits for military training and experience?

- Does the school require you to submit high school official transcripts even if you are transferring in other college credits?

- Can you have your military training and experience evaluated for college credits before you make your final decision?

- Does the school provide Title IV Federal Financial Aid?

- What are the deadlines for the submission of the application, transcripts, other required admissions documents, deposits, accepting your financial aid, etc? All of this information should be readily available on the school's website or directly from the admissions office of the school.

LISTEN UP—IMPORTANT POINT!

During your inquiry into colleges to attend, if at all possible you should plan on scheduling a campus visit to the school. This will provide you the opportunity to see the campus first hand and to visit all of the supporting offices and departments. Prior to

Military student reviewing the admissions process with an admissions counselor. *Author*

visiting, you should ask the admissions staff whether you can complete an application and any other necessary paperwork while you are on campus. This will give you some insight into how the schools treat students. Is it a difficult, bureaucratic process, or do they treat students like customers and provide any visiting potential student with a high degree of customer service?

Apply

Once you have conducted your research and gathered all of the intelligence that you need on each of your school selections and you have made your choice, you will need to formally apply to that college. Make sure that you determine the fee, if any, for submitting your application, before you submit it. Why? Because many colleges waive the application fee for military-related students. If there is a fee, your application will not generally be processed until the fee is received. Once you have applied, you should receive notification, either electronically, via mail, or both, that your application has been received and will be processed accordingly.

During the application process is when you will normally be required to submit your military transcripts for consideration for college transfer credits and any other documents that the school may require. This is where you need to be cautious and a well-informed customer/student. Some schools will require you to take a certain amount of courses/credits with them <u>before</u> they will provide you with an official transfer evaluation of your military and other college credits. A truly military friendly school should provide you with an official transfer evaluation once they have received all of your official documents so it can officially matriculate you into the school.

Completing Your Enrollment

Once you have submitted or the college has received all of the required admissions documents, you should be notified, either electronically and/or through the mail, that "Congratulations you have been accepted."

In general, the acceptance letter will state your required next steps such as completing an intent to enroll form or submitting a Free Application For Federal Student Aid or FAFSA. If you plan on attending as a "resident student," you may also be required to submit medically related forms to verify that you have received certain immunizations. Each state has different requirements for the submission of medical forms and your enrollment or admissions advisor should tell you what you need to do.

One of those "next steps" will be whether or not you will need to submit a deposit to the college or university in order to "hold your seat" in the classroom and in the residence halls (if you plan on living on campus). Many schools

THE BIG IDEA! *Letting your admissions person know that you are a SCS up front is the key to making sure that you are given the opportunity to work with professionals who are familiar with the SCS population and make certain that your benefits will not go to waste!*

January 26, 2010

We are pleased to inform you that you have been accepted as a AS degree candidate in the Accelerated Early Childhood Education program at Post University.

If you are a transfer student, and we have received transcripts from a previous college, a copy of your 'Degree Plan Checklist/Transfer Evaluation' will be mailed to you. This form will indicate how your previous college credits apply to your current degree program at Post University, and the blank spaces will indicate those courses to complete your degree. If you have any questions regarding the transfer evaluation, please contact Kathleen Ring at Kring@post.edu or Julie Horelick at Jhorelick@post.edu.

As an Accelerated Degree Program student, we encourage you to take advantage of academic counseling by contacting the Academic Advising Office by calling 203-596-4646.

Also, enclosed is a Record of Immunization form. This form must be completed *only* if you intend to take classes at any on ground site. Your physician must complete the form and it should be returned to the Post University Health Services Office proving that you have been immuned to/immunized against measles and rubella. By Connecticut state law, you will not be permitted to take classes at any on ground site until this form has been completed and received in the Health Services Office. If you will only be taking classes online, you are not required to return this form.

I am confident that this will be the beginning of an exciting and rewarding experience for you and the University. On behalf of the faculty, staff and the administration, I welcome you to Post University!

Sincerely,

Veronica Marrero, MSM
Director of ADP Admissions

800 Country Club Road • Post Office Box 2540 • Waterbury, CT 06723-2540 • (203) 596-4500

Sample Post University ADP Acceptance Letter. *Post U.*

waive the deposit for military personnel, particularly in online or accelerated programs. However, if you plan on attending as a "resident student" the deposit will, in all likelihood, be required. The deposit can range from $25 to as high as $2,000 for some "prestigious" schools. Before you submit your deposit, make sure you find out when the last day is that you can pull your application and acceptance and still receive a full refund of your deposit. This is normally called the "common response date." This is the date the school has to inform you of your financial aid awards and your financial aid package—allowing you to make a financial decision as to whether or not you can afford to attend the school.

Requesting Financial Aid and/or SCS Educational Benefits

We will cover how to pay for college in a later section of the book. This section is designed to provide you with information on what financial aid is, and where and how it fits into the enrollment process.

Normally, all accredited colleges and universities have the ability to provide need-based financial aid and merit-based scholarships. However, this is not always a given. Make sure that you find out if your intended program of instruction is eligible for financial aid. This is particularly true for vocational programs and schools.

How is need determined? Need is determined by a review of the information provided by you when you complete the FAFSA. To complete the FAFSA, go to www.fafsa.ed.gov. This website will provide you with the step-by-step instructions for completing the application. You will need the FAFSA school code for each college that you are considering attending. The school code for your college(s) should be readily available on the college website under their financial aid pages. You will also be able to search for the school code while completing the FAFSA online. When you complete your FAFSA online, you will receive your EFC—Estimated Family Contribution. Your EFC is the amount of money that the Federal government determines you should be able to contribute to financing your education. The EFC is solely based upon the data that you provided when you completed your FAFSA. The EFC is the primary means of determining how much Federal financial aid you will qualify for. We will go into more detail about the types of federal financial aid in future sections.

NEW UG ADP STUDENT – FINANCIAL AID AWARD LETTER

October 15, 2008

Congratulations on your acceptance to Post University! We have been preparing students for productive careers since 1890, and we are glad to be part of your future. This letter contains important information about **financial aid** to help with your tuition costs. Please read it carefully and get back to us within the timeframe mentioned below to take advantage of this offer.

The Office of Financial Aid has received your FAFSA information from the Department of Education; after review of your information, we are now offering a financial aid award to assist in covering your direct costs of attendance at Post University. For a full-time student (24 credits for the academic award year), the total direct cost of tuition will be $10,200 ($425 per credit hour).

At this time, we are prepared to offer you the following financial aid package for the 2009-2010 academic award year.

Your Estimated Financial Aid Awards

Source:	OCT/JAN	MAR/MAY	Total
Federal Pell Grant Program*	1,750	1,750	3,500
Military Discount Grant	2,100	2,100	4,200
Subsidized Stafford Loan	1,500	1,500	3,000
Total Awards:	5,350	5,350	10,700

NOTE: There will be a 1.5% origination fee deducted from the student's Federal Stafford loan, and a 4% origination fee deducted from the parent's Federal Stafford Plus Loan, prior to disbursement. Your student account will be credited this net amount (not the gross amount shown in your award above).

This award is based on the evaluation of your federal eligibility, financial need, and previously earned college credits. Post University is committed to honoring this award, which is based on the accuracy of the income information submitted, and your matriculation into the University, which includes but is not limited to the receipt of your final official academic transcripts. This award is subject to change, should the aforementioned information change; and awards may be revised accordingly.

Our offer of these financial awards is time-sensitive, and we need to hear back from you within **7 days** of the date on this letter. Our Office of Student Finance will then process your awards and provide information on any additional requirements, such as loan processing, payment plan options, and any other conditions required for federal and state funding.

We are committed to making Post University an affordable choice for preparing you to become a leader in tomorrow's careers, and we are here to assist students and parents with any financing questions that may arise. Please do not hesitate to call your Tuition Planner at the number below.

Your Tuition Planner will be contacting you within 48 hours from the date of this letter to discuss any questions you may have in regards to your awards.

Example of a student financial aid award *Post U.*

Once you submit your FAFSA, it takes about forty-eight hours, or two business days, for the colleges that you indicated on your form to receive your information. Once the school receives your FAFSA data, it will be able to prepare a financial aid award for you. The previous page features an example of a financial aid award.

LISTEN UP—IMPORTANT POINT!

If you are an active member of the military entitled to the tuition assistance program of your branch of service, you may be wondering why you would need to complete a FAFSA. As we discussed in the FTAP section of this chapter, FTA is capped at $750 per course. If you are enrolled in a graduate program (or some undergraduate programs), your FTA may not cover the full tuition costs of your course. If this is your situation, you have a few options. One is to use Federal Financial Aid. The other, if you are eligible for the MGIB-AD Chapter 30 benefit, is to use the "Top-Up Program." (More detail about the MGIB and other funding options will be covered in a later chapter.)

Register

The process for actually registering for your classes will be based on the school and how, either online or as a traditional classroom, you plan on taking your classes. If you will be a "traditional" student, you will probably complete a paper registration form that will be processed by the Office of the Registrar, and then you will be considered registered. If you will be attending as an online student, you will most likely complete an online registration form that again will be processed by the Registrar's Office of your school.

Regardless of the method, before you register, confirm with your admissions counselor that it is alright for you to do so. Many online programs have the ability of placing your student account on "hold" if there is a problem with your student records or your student account with the school. If your account is on hold, you should be notified when you attempt to register. Prompt action on your part if this happens will allow you to quickly resolve the problem and continue your education.

New Students

This section primarily deals with first-time students, but is also for the student who, due to military, family, or work commitments may not have been to school in a long time (periods of ten years or more). You should pay careful attention here if only because the process has inevitably changed since you were last in school (if you have previously attended). This section will also help you in getting back to speed.

Since many schools have strict deadlines to adhere to, it's important to have your paperwork easily accessible. Obviously, your military paperwork should already be saved in a file, but now it's important as a future SCS to have your education information in one separate hard copy file that is always and easily accessible. Scan any documents you have and upload them to your computer. If you can, try to carry a flash drive with you so you have digital copies of all of your paperwork that can be printed on the fly, if it becomes necessary.

Here are some examples of paperwork you should have close at hand for the admissions process:

- **A completed application to the school you are planning on attending**: Like the enlistment papers you completed at the MEPS center or with your recruiter, the application is the gateway to initiating the enrollment process. You can't guarantee your place in any classroom or have your military or previous college credits evaluated without completing an application. Applications usually take no more than fifteen minutes to complete, and rarely more than thirty. These forms used to be filled out by hand and submitted via mail or fax to your enrollment counselor, but now can usually be completed online. The next two pages will demonstrate to you what a typical college application looks like.

- **Military Documents—Orders: (DD-214):** As a SCS, you will in most cases be required to submit documents to verify your status. Examples of these documents may include:

The College Admissions Process

APPLICATION FOR ADMISSIONS
ACCELERATED DEGREE PROGRAM DIVISION – MILITARY PROGRAMS

Email or mail completed application to: Post University Admissions – ADP Division: ATTN: Military Programs, 800 Country Club Road, P.O. Box 2540, Waterbury, CT 06723-2540 email: milprog@post.edu

Questions: Please contact the Military Programs Office at 203-596-4604 OR 203-596-6192 fax: 203-596-8588.

Admission Policy: Admission to Post University is dependent solely upon the applicant's qualifications. Post University does not discriminate on the basis of race, religion, color, sex, national and ethnic origin, or disability in the administration of its educational, admissions, or scholastic and financial assistance policies.

First-time College Students: If you have not previously attended this or any other college, request that your high school forward your official school record to the Office of Admission.

General Equivalency Diploma Holders: Along with your completed Application, you must submit a copy of your Equivalency Diploma and your General Equivalency Diploma test scores to the Office of Admission. All necessary information regarding GED diplomas and scores may be obtained from your State Department of Education Office.

Transfer Students: If you are transferring from a college or university, please ask each institution previously attended to send official transcripts directly to the Admissions Office – Military Programs. Failure to list such institutions on the Application form or to provide transcripts from you must also may be reason for refusal of admission or dismissal. Please note: If you have earned fewer than 12 credits from another institution(s) you must also request an official high school transcript (or GED diploma).

ADMISSIONS DATA: ENTRY TERM: MOD 1 ☐ MOD 2 ☐ MOD 3 ☐ MOD 4 ☐ MOD 5 ☐ MOD 6 ☐

Primary Location (select one): ☐ Online ☐ Waterbury/Main Campus ☐ Meriden ☐ Danbury ☐ West Hartford

Name and Location of Military Installation: _____

Degree Sought: ☐ Associate's Degree ☐ Bachelor's Degree ☐ Masters Degree ☐ Certificate ☐ None*
*Please note: If you are not a candidate for a degree program, transcripts are not required.

How did you hear about Post University? ☐ Briefing ☐ Conference ☐ Co-Worker ☐ ESO ☐ Family Support ☐ Spouse

PERSONAL INFORMATION

☐ Male ☐ Female Social Security Number: ___-___-___ Date of Birth: (mm/dd/yyyy): __/__/__
I AM A DEPENDENT OF A SERVICE MEMBER: ☐ Please indicate below – your spouses' information on their military service and their Pay Basic Entry Date.
Pay Entry Basic Date (PEBD) (month/year) _____

First Name: _____ Middle _____ Last Name: _____

Current Address: (Street) _____

City: _____ State: _____ Zip Code: _____

Email Address: _____

Day Phone: (___)___ Evening Phone: (___)___ Cell Phone: (___)___

Marital Status: ☐ Married ☐ Single ☐ Divorced Maiden Name: _____

Emergency Contact: Name _____ Phone: _____ Relationship: _____

BRANCH OF SERVICE: ☐ ARMY ☐ NAVY ☐ AIR FORCE ☐ MARINES ☐ COAST GUARD
STATUS: ☐ ACTIVE ☐ RESERVE ☐ NATIONAL GUARD ☐ ACTIVE GUARD/RESERVE (AGR) ☐ RETIRED
☐ VETERAN

Will you be applying for: ☐ Federal Tuition Assistance* ☐ GI Bill Benefits ☐ Federal Financial Aid ☐ Employer Tuition Assistance

Name, Location, and Contact Information for your Education Support Office/Specialist: _____

*You must have your Federal Tuition Assistance approved by your Education Office prior to starting your classes. Each Branch of Service has different requirements. Your assigned Enrollment Advisor will provide you with assistance in processing your TA.

Student application, page 1

DEGREE OPTIONS

ASSOCIATE'S DEGREE
- ☐ Accounting
- ☐ Early Childhood Education
- ☐ Legal Studies
- ☐ Management
- ☐ Marketing

CERTIFICATE PROGRAMS
- ☐ Post Baccalaureate - Accounting
- ☐ Computer Information Skills
- ☐ Early Childhood Edu
- ☐ Early Childhood Ed – Admin.
- ☐ HR Management
- ☐ International Business Admin.
- ☐ Paralegal
- ☐ Legal Nurse Counseling

BACCALAUREATE DEGREE
- ☐ Accounting
- ☐ Business Administration*
- ☐ Computer Information Systems (CIS)
- ☐ Criminal Justice
- ☐ Finance
- ☐ Human Services
- ☐ International Business Admin (IBA)
- ☐ Legal Studies
- ☐ Management
- ☐ Marketing

Choose a concentration for the Business Administration Degree:
☐ Accounting ☐ CIS ☐ ECE ☐ Finance ☐ HR ☐ IBA ☐ Legal Studies ☐ Management ☐ Marketing

MASTERS DEGREE
- ☐ HUMAN SERVICES – Clinical Track
- ☐ HUMAN SERVICES – Administrative Track
- ☐ MBA – Entrepreneurship
- ☐ MBA – Corporate Innovation

ACADEMIC HISTORY

Name of High School _____ Telephone (____)_____

City, State, Zip _____

Year of Graduation: _____ Name at time of Attendance: _____

MILITARY EDUCATION HISTORY: (CHECK ALL COURSES THAT YOU HAVE COMPLETED)
☐ PLDC/WLC ☐ BNCOC/ALC ☐ ANCOC/SLC ☐ 1SG/SSC ☐ SGMA ☐ OCS ☐ BOLC ☐ OBC ☐ OAC ☐ CAS³ ☐ C&GSC

List all civilian educational institutions that you attended beyond High School*:

SCHOOL/COURSE	PREVIOUS SURNAME	DATES ATTENDED	CREDITS EARNED	DEGREE(S) RECEIVED

* Please complete a Transcript Request Form for each institution listed

Are you a member of a college honor society? ☐ Yes ☐ No Name of Society: _____

CURRENT EMPLOYER

Name of Employer _____ ☐ Full-time ☐ Part-time _____ # of Years Employed

Address _____ City _____

State _____ Zip Code _____

STATEMENT OF APPLICANT

If admitted, I pledge myself to comply, in good faith, with all the rules and requirements of the University. I realize that any misleading information given by me on this application may be grounds for dismissal.

Applicant's Signature _____ Date ____/____/____

Student application, page 2

A copy of your military orders showing your status (whether you are on active duty, in the reserves, or in the National Guard). Some schools may also require that you submit a copy of your Military ID Card.

Are you a veteran? If so, you will need to provide a copy of your DD-214 showing the type of separation that you received. The DD-214 shows your eligibility for VA benefits, but also may provide assistance to an academic advisor as they work to transfer your military training and experience into college credits. Military dependents who may be using their service members veterans benefits may be required to submit a copy of the service member's DD-214 as well.

Note: Some institutions may require that your DD-214 be notarized for the purpose of verifying your military status. This can be done at your local town or city hall, or just contact a local private notary.

- **An unofficial copy of your military training transcripts specific to your branch of the service (AARTS, SMART, etc.)**: This is especially vital in determining the amount of credits you may be eligible for through your military training. May also be used for service verification by some institutions.

- **For the dependent and spouse, proof of your relationship to the person whose benefits you are receiving**: This verification can include, but is not limited to, things like tax returns, marriage certificates, and copies of dependent identification cards.

- **Immunization records (if you are attending classes on campus)**: Most colleges require immunization records for admission to classes on campus. If you are in the military, these can be readily obtained at your unit; civilians can make a trip to the doctor, who will help you prepare these before the start of class.

- **Any paperwork specific to the university (transcript request forms, declaration of major forms)**: Each

TRANSCRIPT REQUEST FORM
Office of Student Information

Dear Student,

In order to complete the application process, the admissions committee must have an official transcript from all previous educational institutions you have attended. For your convenience, please:

1. Complete the Authorization for Release of Information form below.
2. Mail, fax, or personally deliver to the appropriate college/universities, and in turn the official transcripts will be forwarded directly to Post.

The final official high school transcripts must include: **Date of graduation, seal and signature**
All transcripts must be mailed from the previous school you attended, to: **Post University**

Thank you for your prompt attention to this matter. Should you have any questions concerning the application process, please feel free to contact the Office of Admissions at 1-800-345-2562.

Sincerely,
Jay Murray
Director of Admissions

Authorization For Release of Information

I HEREBY GIVE PERMISSION TO: _____
(Name of current or previous school)

TO RELEASE TRANSCRIPTS TO: Post University, Office of the Registrar
800 Country Club Road, P.O. Box 2540
Waterbury, CT 06723-2540

Name of current or previous school _____
Address _____
Date(s) Attended _____
Your Telephone No. _____   Social Security No. _____
Print Last Name _____   First Name _____
Address _____
City _____   State _____ Zip Code _____
Your Signature _____   Date _____

Rev. 08

University transcript request form. *Post U.*

university has its own protocol for paperwork it requires for admission into a program. Most universities have applications and similar forms you can obtain and submit online, and virtually all forms, from transcript request forms to recommendation letter forms, are available online as well. (A sample form is shown above.)

The College Admissions Process

THE BIG IDEA! *Have all your files ready for the admissions process before actually beginning it. Scrounging around for papers at the last minute wastes time and delays the process and may ultimately delay obtaining your educational goals or discourage them altogether.*

Transfer Students

If you have been to another college previously before the one you are going through the admissions process with, and have credits to show for it, you will be considered a "transfer student." If you are a student who has obtained a degree previously and is looking for another degree or certification, you should also consider yourself a transfer student, even if you attended the same school for your prior degree. Why? Because you often need to follow the same steps, in some cases to include obtaining official transcripts from that same school.

The items transfer students need to have ready are as follows:

- **Unofficial copies of all transcripts from any previous colleges you wish to have credits evaluated from**: If you are a student transferring your credits in from another institution, this is a very important process in verifying your previous education up to this point. Get in the habit of requesting <u>four transcripts</u> if you have to move on from an institution as a student and you want to finish your degree at another institution or at another time. One of these may be opened by yourself and kept as a hard copy and scanned and kept as a digital file, keeping in mind that this now renders the transcript unofficial for the purpose of most admissions departments. If you still have student ID access to a prior institution, most will allow you to print an unofficial copy of your transcripts online while you are still a student there.

- **Official copies of all schools you wish to have credits evaluated from**: When you leave a school, you should request no fewer than <u>three copies</u> in sealed envelopes provided by the Registrar besides any copies you wish to use for your printed records. Do this for every school you wish to have credits evaluated from. Keep in mind you can never be sure of which credits will transfer to which school until an advisor looks at them. Most schools require a letter grade of "C" or better for transferring in credits; some will allow grades of "P" on the pass-fail grading system. Keep in mind that not having the official transcripts ready at an early enough time may delay the admissions process while you wait for your transcripts, so have them ready well in advance.

* Note: *Some schools require a certain cumulative GPA (Grade Point Average) in the subject area you plan to study or from the entirety of your transcripts. Check with your admissions counselor for further details. Admissions departments typically do not accept an opened transcript (removed from sealed envelope) as official. Keep your official transcripts sealed!*

- **Individual program requirements (letters of recommendation, resumes)**: You will typically need these for advanced degree programs, particularly those of a professional nature. Pay special attention to the specific requirements of each program in regards to these documents. Some programs are looking for an updated professional resume to verify your background and experience if they are requiring it as part of the admissions process. Other programs require letters of recommendation. Be careful and make sure you obtain the type of recommendations the school is looking for. Some require academic recommendations (from a professor or university supervisor), some require professional recommendations (military or civilian supervisors), and some accept them from any source that can verify your potential success as a student in the field you are applying for.

- **Entrance exams and standardized tests**: Again, mostly for the SCS applying for graduate programs, though for younger students applying to traditional colleges you may be required to produce SAT scores. These professional tests used to determine admissions in schools include the GRE (Graduate

Readiness Exam), GMAT (Graduate Management Admissions Test), or the LSAT (Law School Admission Test). Be sure to have official copies of your test results handy, and keep them as you would your transcripts.

- *Course descriptions*: If you recall, we mentioned in the previous chapter that at times you may have courses that will not transfer in from one school to another. Often there is a perfectly good reason for this. However, sometimes your academic advisors working on evaluating your transfer credits may come across a class they do not recognize. Therefore, you may have to provide documentation from the university you attended to verify the nature of the course so the advisor can properly determine whether or not the credits are transferrable. The online site for the colleges you attended previously should have a description of the course(s) taken available online, or one should be available in the form of a brief paragraph or a syllabus by contacting the academic advisor for the school you attended previously. Of course, you shouldn't be expected to have this documentation ready for every class you took, but you should be prepared to know who to contact at your prior school and be able to find the information relatively quickly should the need arise.

Matriculation and Registration

Now that you've been through the admissions process, you are probably ready to matriculate. I know that sounds like an intimidating word—something a drill sergeant might yell at you! "Private, you'd better matriculate when I tell you to, or I'll have you doing pushups until it hurts!"

Matriculation isn't really a scary word at all. Matriculation describes the process by which the school handles the paperwork you submitted and thus prepares you on the path to obtaining a degree or certificate. Basically, matriculation is little more than an administrative green light that accepts you so you can get down to business. Once you submit your aforementioned paperwork to the standards required by the institution you want to attend, you will be processed for matriculation by the admissions staff. The process usually culminates with your advisors

THE BIG IDEA! As a transfer student you may be worn out from having been through the admissions process before and consider it a daunting task. However, you should use your experience to your advantage. Preparing yourself early on in the process is important and will help ensure your transition into your new school a smooth one!

receiving your paperwork and collaborating with you on the path to obtaining your certificate or degree.

In some cases you may find yourself taking classes at another institution on a temporary basis. Example: Before you obtain your degree from College X, you move to another duty station. There, you decide you want to take a course or two at College Y so you can complete your degree, or take courses online while you are deployed overseas so you don't fall too far behind in your education goals at your home school. In cases like these where you only need a few courses, you can take classes as a "non-matriculated" student who is not seeking a degree with that institution. This is ideal for taking only a few courses in any number of areas to fulfill your requirements elsewhere.

However, be sure to confirm with your academic advisor at your home school to be certain the courses you are taking at your temporary institution are eligible for transfer and meet the requirements for the degree you are seeking, or else, you are simply wasting your time!

LISTEN UP—IMPORTANT POINT!

The registration process for your class or classes can greatly vary between institutions depending upon the guidelines at the school you are attending. Just because one school did things a certain way in the past, don't assume that every other school does things just the same way!

In some cases, schools allow students to register in person at the Registrar or Admissions Office. Some schools allow students to register online themselves, if not at first for their initial courses, then further along in the process.

Just about every degree program has courses that are required to be taken first before any other classes. These are called "prerequisites," and should be treated as an important step for you to take before advancing deeper in your subject area. Some programs require taking certain courses (prerequisites) before being accepted into a program. Your academic advisor or admissions counselor, of course, should clearly communicate this to you before you register. Either way, do not try to circumvent the system: you will have plenty of opportunities to take the courses you want at a later time!

Lastly, be mindful to take note of specifically what courses you have been registered for and what the section number is and the date the courses start and end—particularly if you are utilizing tuition assistance (TA). This information will be crucial when applying for TA to make sure the school is properly paid for the courses you are taking.

University Admissions Office

> *Note: If you are using the GoArmyEd/EArmyU tuition assistance system, be aware that some schools enable you to register for courses directly through the GoArmyEd/EArmyU web portal, while others require you to register there and through the school for your courses.*

THE BIG IDEA! *Getting registered for your first classes will seem a bit challenging at first. However, if you collaborate with your admissions counselor and academic advisor along the way and use them as your guides, you will soon be ready to start your classes!*

Getting Ready

Now that your first classes are set, there really isn't that much left you need to do. But what's is left to do is important! [Of course, preparing to pay for your education is important. It's so important, we've dedicated an entire chapter on it later in the book!]

One of the most important things to work on before you start your classes is an assessment of your technology, particularly for those of you engaged in an online or distance-learning program. For the benefit of the SCS reading this book who haven't been to school in some time, computers are now an absolutely vital part of the higher education experience. Two decades ago, you took a standard introductory to computer course for a curriculum requirement to prepare for using them in the business world. You used computer labs for typing papers, and that was about it.

Since then, however, college campuses and academic programs have become showcases of the latest and greatest technical advances. Almost every campus now has WiFi Internet access. This allows you to wirelessly connect to the Internet anywhere on campus as a guest or with your student ID. The online course and program offerings are cutting-edge, requiring you to learn to use any number of programs designed to host an online classroom. It goes without saying that you should be certain to have at least a basic knowledge of modern computers before engaging in such a program. None of this is very hard to learn, but you have to prepare for it in advance.

Even if you are participating in a program on campus, if you are planning on using your own computer, now is a good time to make sure both your computer hardware and software is updated. If you don't have a reliable computer or accommodations to use one at your workstation or access to your school's campus (nearly every campus has public computer access of some sort available to students free of charge), you should consider updating your existing computer or purchasing a new one before you commit to making the leap into the admissions process.

* * *

LISTEN UP—IMPORTANT POINT!

Double check and update your gear! We recommend that you consider buying a laptop or notebook computer rather than a traditional tower desktop. The difference between desktops and laptops in terms of power, capabilities, and price are no longer an issue, and many laptops now offer the power and storage of a desktop unit for about the same price. Laptops, however, offer more flexibility than a traditional desktop and, if you plan on using your computer on campus or at any number of locations from coffee shops to public libraries, you will find WiFi hotspots that could save you hundreds of dollars a year on internet service. Laptops will also come in handy for lectures because you can take your laptop to class and document lectures in a neat and organized manner. You can also plug in to present Excel® and PowerPoint® files to classmates for presentations. Some programs, particularly professional graduate programs, may require you to purchase a laptop for the program before participating. The computers are leased or purchased outright and usually come with service contracts to protect them against damage and additional software indigenous to the program. Be sure to discuss the details of this with your admissions counselor.

If you have a reliable computer setup already, make sure your printer is also updated. Printer / scanner / copier combinations are now relatively inexpensive and are vital for printing up syllabi, making digital copies of your professor's corrections, and scanning copies of your personal paperwork or items for your portfolio. Software updates are also important. Be sure you have the latest versions of programs such as Adobe Acrobat® and Microsoft Office®, which are vital for helping you download and produce documents for research and present assignments to instructors and your classmates. If you are an Apple/Mac® user, be certain that any school files pertaining to admissions or assignments in the future are saved in files compatible with Windows® format. Be sure to ask your professor for details on these points.

Remember when we told you earlier to keep track of what courses you were registered for? Well, this will certainly come in handy during the first week or two of school. If you are a student attending courses on campus, your schedule will help you navigate where you need to be on campus and when you need to be there. Additionally, you also can use your course schedule to contact your instructor a few days early to obtain your syllabus and ask for some tips on success for the course. Finally, you will also need a copy of your course schedule to order books from the bookstore. Many bookstores are on campus. Some online schools allow you to order books online, where they are shipped directly to you. Either way, make sure you are ordering books for the correct section, as several sections have different books for the same subject depending upon the instructor.

If you are a student on campus, you may have to bring the aforementioned immunization form to the campus medical facility for verification. Some universities also will require you to fill out an insurance form, to offer protection of the university's liability if you are ill or injured on campus. If you have insurance through another carrier or insurance with the VA, it's a good idea to get in the habit of carrying your card with you if you don't already. Be prepared to offer this as verification of your coverage.

If you are attending classes on campus or live close enough to the campus where you intend to spend some time there, take a walk around for a day or part of a day before getting started. Be sure to get a student ID to allow full access to the campus, and be sure to carry it with you at all times and, like your military ID, be prepared to show it to a school official for verification at any time. Get to know the location of the main points on campus like the student center, the library, and places to eat if you will be on campus for any extended period of time. Ask a student liaison or your admissions counselors to see what perks you may be eligible for. Many schools offer use of their gyms, which often feature state-of-the-art equipment for NCAA athletic programs and world class research libraries. Showing your school ID may even offer you discounts to merchants around the campus. Take full advantage of these benefits if you commute or live on or near campus.

Finally, regardless of what type of school you're attending, you'll probably want to find out where you can find some gear for your school. Usually found in catalogs, the campus bookstore, or online through the university athletic website, a sweatshirt, t-shirt, or cap representing the university will give you a sense of belonging in much the same way clothing representing the branch of service you are (or were) in makes you feel. These also make great gifts for holidays and birthdays and allow your family and friends to share in the excitement of your new journey by showing their support of your education. Wearing the gear yourself you'll develop *esprit de corps* when you run into fellow students or alumni in town. Likewise, when on campus, don't be afraid to show off your service swag: not only might it help you strike up a conversation with classmates, but it might help introduce you to other SCS on campus. Either way, wear your colors proudly!

THE BIG IDEA! *Once you are registered, classes will be here before you know it. Prepare yourself early to ensure personal success, and save the stress for your first test and paper! Show off your school pride by proudly embracing your latest assignment—Service Connected Student!*

CHAPTER 6

How Do I Pay for College?

"An investment in knowledge always pays the best interest."
— Benjamin Franklin

Paying for College

As a SCS, you have a number of programs at your disposal in order to fund your college education. Federal Tuition Assistance programs, Montgomery GI Bill Educational Benefits, Title IV Federal Financial Aid, Civilian Career Accounts, and employer tuition reimbursement benefits are among the most common programs available to you for funding your education. Because the majority of these programs are funded by the federal government, understanding the rules and regulations that govern these programs can be a daunting task.

The purpose of this section of the book is not to make you a subject matter expert in all of these programs. Rather, its purpose is to provide you with enough information so that when you are speaking to a so-called subject matter expert at financial aid offices, you know what questions to ask them.

LISTEN UP—IMPORTANT POINT!

If you are still serving in the military, you have a number of options available to you that include your branch of service's Federal Tuition Assistance Program, the GI Bill, and Federal Title IV Financial Aid.

Federal Tuition Assistance Programs

The Federal Tuition Assistance Program (FTAP) is the one form of education benefit that does not vary among the various federal branches of the service, and does not change whether you are on active duty or reserve status. Regardless of which branch of the service you sign up for, you are eligible for the same version of the government's tuition assistance payment program, which, at the time of publication, is set at $250 per credit hour, or $166.67 per quarter hour for a maximum payout of $750 per course. FTAP is also available for vocational and technical schools, and pays a total of $16.67 per clock hour. This amount is the maximum amount allowable per course, and a total of $4,500 per year is allocated to each member of the *federal* military to be used (National Guard will be explained). This is available regardless of rank or classification. There is typically no requirement for enlistment to utilize tuition assistance. In other words, you do not have to agree to any additional service to your country to utilize this aspect of financial aid, and you are not required to use it at any point in time in your contract. However, if you are an officer, you may be required to have a certain amount of time left on your contract. And when you are no longer affiliated with the service either through ETS or retirement, you will no longer be eligible for tuition assistance (TA).

Tuition assistance is available at $4,500 at the beginning of each fiscal year (the program regenerates itself every October, when the fiscal year starts again). This allows you the ability to take six traditional courses while utilizing federal tuition assistance. However, there is one thing to remember: ***tuition assistance is a privilege, and not a right***.

Typically, there are individual deadlines for applying for tuition assistance set forth by branches of service or commands. Be proactive and apply early for it, well before your class starts if at all possible. Failure to obtain it in a timely manner could lead to non-payment and could incur unexpected out-of-pocket costs to you. In some service branches, there are pay-grade requirements to ask permission of the unit commander before applying for TA. For example, in the Army, E-6 or lower must seek their commander's approval to procure TA, and must provide documentation to verify this in the form of a DA-2171. Other branches may have similar forms and requirements; check with your unit commander.

LISTEN UP—IMPORTANT POINT!

Tuition assistance is just that. It can't be applied to cover anything beyond the cost of tuition. It is paid directly to the school, so the funds do not come to you directly. The amount of $4,500 does not change no matter how high your tuition costs are. Keep that in mind.

Depending on your branch of the service or your status, you may be able to use your GI Bill concurrently to "top off" your tuition. In other words, if your tuition is in excess of the $750 limit, you may be able to use your GI Bill to cover the difference. However, it is often the case that the annual total of the TA must be expended first in order to utilize the GI Bill. On the flip side, members of the military are typically able to receive their GI Bill simultaneously. Check with your ESO for details on the rules for TA specific to your status and branch of service.

The National Guard warrants its own topic of discussion. It is important to note that the Air and Army National Guard are both under federal *and* state jurisdiction. What this means to you as a member is that some states are pooled in with the budgets of the federal tuition assistance, while others have their own in-state pooled budgets for education. Therefore, your National Guard benefits can and will vary greatly from state to state. Additionally, because there may be a limited budget for TA, it is extremely important to apply for it as soon as possible. Each state also has its own methods of paying tuition assistance for its National Guard and the availability of funds should be verified. Be sure to check with your unit commander or State Education Officer for more details.

A word about eligibility. Keep in mind again that TA is not a right. Your TA, unlike your GI Bill, has a requirement to maintain a 2.0 (C-letter) average or higher in order to maintain your tuition eligibility. Failure to maintain that GPA requirement means a number of penalties, including but not limited to, the following:

- *Revoking of TA privileges*—If your GPA dips below a 2.0, you will not be eligible for additional TA through the service.

- *Payment for classes*—Depending on policy, you may find that you are forced to pay for your classes you took previously.

TA can be reinstated if a course is retaken and a satisfactory GPA is achieved, or if the GPA is brought up through taking other courses. Keep in mind that TA won't be available while taking these courses. Therefore, other sources of benefits, such as the GI Bill, will have to be used in order to bridge the gap.

Obtaining Tuition Assistance

Although each branch of the service has an equal amount of TA available to each member, each has its own way of paying those funds. For the most part, following the above protocol of contacting your unit commander and local ESO will help you follow the steps and assist you with the documentation needed to procuring your TA and pay your school. Also, the following websites feature TA applications for each branch of the service:

Coast Guard:
www.uscg.mil/HQ/CGI/cfa/ta.asp

Marine Corps/Navy:
www.navycollege.navy.mil/nta.cfm

National Guard:
www.virtualarmory.com/education/fedbenefits/tuition_fta.aspx

Electronic Applications for the Army and Air Force: The Future of Obtaining TA

The sites listed above use antiquated documentation, which means miles of red tape to apply for TA for each SCS. The same is not true for the Army or the Air Force, which have both created a computer-based system to streamline the application process and eliminate paper applications. This avoids the lines at ESOs to apply for TA and brings the process to the airman or soldier, who now can be responsible for obtaining TA on their own.

The Army's system was developed earlier in the decade, when the need to bring the application for education benefits to the modern era was realized. The creation of the GoArmyEd Education portal was a welcome change for soldiers, ESOs, and college administrators alike as it greatly streamlined the process of applying for TA, eliminating red tape in the process. It is a model that, while not perfect, is a great improvement over what was in place before. As college administrators, we sincerely hope other branches of the service will follow suit.

While it can be a bit daunting at first to set up, you will quickly find that the process makes applying for tuition assistance a relatively painless effort once the system is properly in place. Since we are encountered with many questions from first-time users of GoArmyEd on how to set up an account and download a class, we have dedicated this section to assisting the soldier SCS with obtaining TA step-by-step on GoArmyEd's system.

To set up your GoArmyEd account, you are required to start with the following four steps:

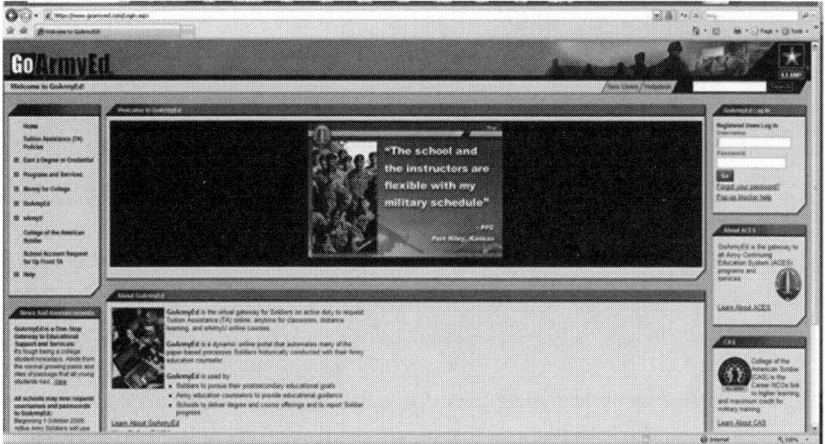

1. Obtain permission from your commander, if necessary, to use TA.

2. Use your AKO login to create your GoArmyEd account.

3. Complete the Common Application.

4. Have your ESO change your home school to the institution of your choice. This step is critical in making sure the coursework has been loaded into your GoArmyEd account from the institution you are selecting.

Once these steps are completed, you can begin the steps to applying for your TA.

The steps are as follows:

1. Select the "Earn a Degree or Credential" link located in the left menu of your homepage.

2. A new window opens and the Search Course Schedule screen displays. Enter your school, and next to "subject" put the three letter course designator (for example, ENG for English). Hit "search" at the bottom of the screen.

3. Choose the correlating class section. Look for the part in the upper left column of the selection by the green dot that says "Class Nbr." Copy that number (4-5 digits) and save it.

4. Return to the GoArmyEd homepage. From that homepage, select the "Enroll or Drop / Withdraw from a Course" link in the My Virtual Education Center section.

5. Select "Request TA and Enroll In a Course."

6. When the Statement of Understanding appears, read the document. Click Yes to acknowledge agreement to the terms (if you agree) and enter your password before hitting submit.

7. Verify your account information to ensure that all fields are updated to reflect your current location. Select the "Account Information Verified" button to accept. Select "OK" when the pop-up message appears, then select "Continue."

8. Then the "Select Classes to add" screen comes up. Select the appropriate term and enter the 4 or 5-digit number you copied previously into the "Enter Class Nbr" column on the left side of the page.

9. After hitting "enter," the course should appear under "my pending enrollments." Click the button that says "Process Step 2 of 3."

10. At this point the "Confirm classes" screen should display. It should say "Student Amount" for the remainder not covered under TA (if any) and the GoArmyEd Amount should be the amount TA will cover for your particular course.

If you have any questions regarding GoArmyEd, your assigned ESO will be happy to help you. Just ask.

On the heels of the Army's GoArmyEd TA application system, the Air Force created its own system—its education portal. Because the Air Force's system was recently released, we were unable to obtain visuals of the website before the publication of this book. The steps necessary to complete the process are relatively similar to the Army's.

1. Select the reason you are requesting TA. There are four options available. Pick the one that suits you best.

2. Select the school you will be attending. Select from the list available. If your school is not on the list, please contact your ESO at once.

3. Select the start date of your course. Bear in mind the dates may not exactly match the start dates of your school. If the term is incorrect, tuition assistance may not be approved.

4. Insert course information. The course information for your school should be loaded in by your ESO prior to you applying for TA, which will make your search easier as the courses will show up in an additional window on the site. However, if this is not the case, you can search for a course by inputting information on the course from the institution itself.

5. Enter the fees for the course.

6. Verify the information for the TA applied for and submit.

The Air Force online TA application can be reached through their education portal, available at www.my.af.mil/

THE BIG IDEA! *Federal Tuition Assistance provides the active reserve SCS with a great opportunity to help defray the cost of tuition to college. Be sure to take advantage of it while you are in the service—once you leave, it's gone!*

The GI Bill

There were two driving purposes behind the creation of the GI Bill: necessity and appreciation. The GI Bill has become synonymous with education benefits for military personnel, and it is, dollar-for-dollar, arguably the single most important benefit that active duty military members can sign for. It can help you both in your career while you are in the military and, unlike most perks related with military service, you can not only continue to utilize it when you leave the service, but don't have to retire from the service in order to continue using this important benefit. In some cases, you can even *transfer* it to your dependents!

The GI Bill was originally titled the Serviceman's Readjustment Act of 1944 by President Franklin Roosevelt. It was created to help veterans returning home from World War II. The debate regarding the GI Bill in the 1940s was centered on two main topics. Many felt that paying an unemployed veteran $20 per week would lessen their motivation to seek employment. Others did not see the benefit of sending combat veterans to colleges and universities, as this was viewed (in that era) as a privilege reserved for the rich.

In 1966, President Lyndon Johnson took it one step further with the Veteran's Readjustment Benefits Act of 1966. Now, all military veterans who served in wartime or peace could receive these benefits. This eventually led to the formation of the Montgomery GI Bill in 1984, which has existed in various forms since, each divided into chapters to identify them. The following pages examine some of these chapters.

Chapter 30

Known as the present-day Montgomery GI Bill for active duty, service members, Chapter 30 allows forfeiture of $100 of pay for 12 months to receive a payout for education. This amount has variances depending on when the student decides to use the GI Bill, and whether he or she is at full-time or part-time status. They may use the benefits for college, vocational courses, or specific job training, and the benefits last for up to 36 months for active duty service. At the present time, this version of the GI Bill comes with an option to add on additional benefits in the form of an added $600 "kicker." For every dollar contributed toward the kicker, the government offers another $8, meaning that when the service member leaves the service, he can have an additional $5,400 at his disposal. The service member can use his GI Bill benefits while in service to add to the tuition assistance, but may also use it when he leaves the service as well. This benefit, however, must be used before 10 years after their ETS. However, he may be eligible for additional time for certain difficulties, such as a service-connected disability. The MGIB program pays for tuition and fees above TA cap, called a "top-up."

LISTEN UP—IMPORTANT POINT!

One important thing to remember is that the GI Bill is paid directly to the student and not the school in the form of a check from the Treasury Department. You are free to use the money to pay for whatever you wish pertaining to your studies—books, tuition, student fees, etc. But remember the onus to pay the bill is on you: the VA does not pay for your education directly.

Here are some specific categories for eligibility for the Chapter 30 GI Bill:

Category I:

- You must have entered active duty for the first time after June 30, 1985;

- Had your military pay reduced by $100 a month for the first 12 months of your enlistment contract;

- You continuously served for three years, or two years (based on your enlistment contract), or two years if you entered into the Selected Reserve within one year of leaving active duty and served 4 years.

Category II:

- You entered active duty before January 1, 1977;

- You served at least one day between 10/19/1984 and 6/30/1985, and stayed on active duty through 6/30/1988, or 6/30/1987 if you entered the Selected Reserve within one year of leaving active duty and served four years;

- You had benefits remaining from the Vietnam-Era GI Bill on 12/31/1989.

Category III:

- You are not eligible under either Category I or II;

- You were on active duty on 9/30/1990 and you were involuntarily separated after 2/2/1991;

- Or you were involuntarily separated on or after 11/30/1993;

- Or you voluntarily separated under the VSI or SSB program;

- Before separation you contributed through military payroll reduction $1,200.

Category IV:

- You were on active duty on 10/9/1996 AND you had money remaining in a VEAP account AND you elected the MGIB by 10/9/1997;

- Or you became a full-time National Guardsmen, under the USC Title 32 AG/R program between 7/1/1985 and 11/28/1989 and you selected the MGIB between the period of 10/9/1996 and 7/8/1997;

- You had your pay reduced by $100 per month for 12 months or made a $1,200 lump sum contribution.

If you have any questions regarding you eligibility, please contact the VA.

Chapter 31

The Vocational Rehabilitation component of the Montgomery GI Bill (Chapter 31) is for veterans or service members who have *service-connected disabilities*. These benefits require a certain amount of disability, either 10% minimum for veterans, or 20% for active duty. This version requires the service member to first be rated at that level of disability in order to be able to declare vocational rehab benefits, and allows for more time—12 years or more, depending upon circumstances—to utilize these benefits than the Chapter 30 benefits.

If you have any questions regarding you eligibility, please contact the VA.

Chapter 32

The Veterans Education Assistance Program (VEAP) initially served as the first version of the pay-in GI Bill benefits. Under this plan, the service member, who enlisted between January 1, 1977, and June 30, 1985, paid into an education plan and were matched $2 for every $1 they put in by the federal government. For determination of your eligibility, please contact the VA.

Chapter 33

The Chapter 33 GI Bill benefits, or the Post-9/11 GI Bill, is probably the reason many of you have purchased this book. It is, without question the single largest veterans' initiative for education made by the U.S. government since the Vietnam War.

With this plan, the federal government has changed the rules to alter both the methods of payment to the SCS and the availability of this payout. This plan now allows three key SCS populations reading this book—veterans, Reservists, and dependents—access to the kind of GI Bill benefits that may have originally benefitted active duty personnel in the past. This benefit is clearly designed to reflect the changing dynamics of war in the United States in the new millennium and the erosion of "weekend warrior" Reservists who once were commonplace among the branches of the service. Gone are the days where a Reservist could, in theory, retire after 20 years of service without serving on active duty with the exception of training. Now, even a short three- to six-year enlistment period as a Reservist is a virtual guarantee of at least some time deployed on active duty—quite possibly to one of the front lines of the current wars in the Middle East. This is a reflection that the dedication and sacrifices of our service members since 9/11 has gone above and beyond what anyone could have foreseen in the relatively docile post-Cold War era in the years prior.

On August 1, 2009, this version of the GI Bill was unveiled and a growing number of eligible service members and veterans have applied for it. Here are some of the remarkable benefits from this form of the GI Bill that make it <u>different</u> from any prior GI Bill initiative:

- The benefits are available effective August 1, 2009, the date when the program began. If a student is no longer active, he may still be eligible for his benefits and does not need to perform additional military duty in order to receive the benefits;

- Although considered benefits acquired through active duty service, these benefits *are not* a pay-in plan. There is no payment required for these benefits to be used;

- This bill is *not* eligible for those still serving on active duty. This means that these are active duty-size payments available to veterans and Reservists—*even those who weren't serving when the bill was created.*

- The benefits are not a lump-sum payment, but rather in four different sections: An initial up-front payment to help with start-up costs such as applications and supplies, a yearly stipend for books, tuition payment, and a BAH allowance for housing;

- The amount available for tuition and for housing is dependent upon the geographic location of the SCS at the time of using the benefit;

- Part of the payment is paid directly to school for tuition, while additional stipends and payments go to the SCS directly;

- The SCS has 15 years from the time they leave the service to utilize this unique benefit rather than 10 years for other GI Bill benefit.

LISTEN UP—IMPORTANT POINT!

For anyone who served a minimum of 90 days on active duty after September 11, 2001, they are eligible for the following benefits from the post-9/11 GI Bill:

- Tuition and fees, paid to the highest in-state per credit for tuition rate. See link below. This is paid directly to the institution of choice based on the number of hours you are certified for;

- A one-time payment equaling $500 to cover start-up costs for certain individuals;

- A stipend of $1,000 per academic year to use on books, prorated based upon your number of courses;

- Basic Allowance Housing (BAH) payment to the student equivalent to E-5 pay *determined by the location of the school they are attending.* This may be used to cover expenses associated to rent and mortgage and is not contingent upon the student living on campus. Please follow the link below to determine BAH rate for your school;

- ***Note: The BAH benefit for the post-9/11 GI Bill benefit is <u>not</u> available as of the time of publication to students attending a wholly online program!** Students who wish to take classes online may qualify for the BAH benefit by taking a minimum of 51% of their curriculum requirements at the site of the school they are attending, or at another institution that will transfer in credits towards the degree they are pursuing. For an updated list of BAH rates for the location of the school you will be attending, please go to the following helpful link on the Veterans' Administration website: www.defensetravel.dod.mil/perdiem/bah.html

These benefits are eligible to any active military member, veteran, or Reservist who served on active duty for a minimum of 90 days after 9/11. Here is the breakdown of time that you served and a percentage of the above benefits you may be eligible for:

TIME ON ACTIVE DUTY AFTER SEPTEMBER 11, 2001	PERCENTAGE OF THE BENEFIT AVAILABLE:
90 -180 DAYS	40%
6-12 MONTHS	50%
12-18 MONTHS	60%
18-24 MONTHS	70%
24-30 MONTHS	80%
30-36 MONTHS	90%
36 MONTHS AND OVER	100%

Department of Veterans Affairs

What this means is a lot of money in pocket and—thanks to your service during one of the most difficult times in our nation's history—some additional benefits the previous versions of the GI Bill may not have offered you.

For further information on the new post-9/11 GI Bill and to help determine eligibility, please go to this link on the VA website: www.gibill.va.gov/GI_Bill_Info/benefits.htm#CH33

Yellow Ribbon Program

If all these benefits are not enough reason to consider the Chapter 33 version of the GI Bill, for those of you who qualified for the 36 months of active duty, or 100% of the GI Bill benefit, things get even better. As a provision to the bill, the Yellow Ribbon Program was created to add to the tuition benefits of the post-9/11 GI Bill.

The Yellow Ribbon Program allows the SCS to use the GI Bill at a school with tuition higher than the rate of the highest state school. Under the Yellow Ribbon Program, the school will fund 50% of the education of the student for the amount above the tuition level set by the post-9/11 GI Bill, and the VA will fund the remainder of the balance.

What does this mean to you as an SCS who meets the criteria and is considering the post-9/11 GI Bill? It means you will be able to go to the institution of your choice—provided it is an active participant in the program—without regard to tuition, knowing that your tuition rate will be covered, and you won't have to utilize alternate means to pay the difference. In the past, you may have had to consider another school because of the tuition amount. Today, if that institution is a Yellow Ribbon Program school, you can attend without worrying about how to pay tuition, comforted in the knowledge that the school and the VA will pay for the difference.

Many schools across the country have already joined the Yellow Ribbon Program and are helping post-9/11 GI Bill students use their benefits to their fullest. To see if one of the schools you are interested in is a Yellow Ribbon Program school, use this link to find the list on the VA website: www.gibill.va.gov/GI_Bill_Info/CH33/YRP/YRP_List.htm

Chapter 35

The Survivors and Dependents' Education Assistance Program allows education benefits for dependents of veterans who are fully disabled on a permanent basis or perished due to a service-related incident. These benefits are eligible to be used for the same type of programs as the other VA education benefits. However, they are eligible for 45 months, rather than the former 36 months. Any dependent utilizing these VA benefits must go through the VA to obtain them as with an SCS who served. To determine eligibility, please follow this link to the VA's main page: www.gibill.va.gov/GI_Bill_Info/benefits.htm

Chapter 1606

This chapter and the one that follows deal specifically with the programs available to Reservists. This particular chapter, known as the Selected Reserve Montgomery GI Bill, includes Reservists in all branches of the federal service, as well as the National Guard and Air National Guard. In this version of the GI Bill, the service member *does not* need to contribute money to receive a payment. In some cases, he or she may also be eligible for additional "top-offs" or "kickers," just like the traditional GI Bill. However, because there is no buy-in, the payment for these GI Bill payments tends to be significantly less, at this time about one-quarter of the payment of the traditional GI Bill on a monthly basis.

Unlike the traditional GI Bill, however, there are no restrictions to utilizing the GI Bill in conjunction with TA benefits. This allows the GI Bill to be used for added tuition payment or additional expenses, such as student fees or books, immediately.

Here are some criteria for eligibility:

- You have a six-year commitment to serve in the Selected Reserve signed after June 30, 1985;

- You must complete your initial active duty for training requirements (basic training and your military job school);

- Meet the requirement of earning a high school diploma or GED before completing your IADT;

- Remain in good standing while serving in an active Selected Reserve unit.

If you have any questions regarding your eligibility, please see your unit commander or go online and follow this link to the VA website: www.gibill.va.gov/GI_Bill_Info/benefits.htm

Chapter 1607

This particular chapter also deals with Reservists, but like the post-9/11 GI Bill, it offers an added benefit. For many, having spent time as a Reservist often leaves you limited options in terms of payout—a few months at most. However, Chapter 1607 enables the SCS to obtain a portion of the benefits of the traditional active duty Montgomery GI Bill in exchange for 90 consecutive days of active duty service after September 11, 2001. This enables them to take a benefit equivalent to 80% of the payout of the active duty GI Bill *provided they remain in the military in some capacity.* To determine eligibility, please follow this link to the VA website: www.gibill.va.gov/GI_Bill_Info/benefits.htm

Changing Chapters of the GI Bill

There are various ways for a service member to change his or her GI Bill benefits from one chapter to another, or to add on to current benefits. Here are some examples of applicable scenarios:

- Students who used 36 months of reserve or active GI Bill benefits can add to their benefits by changing their duty status. For example, a student who used all 36 months of their active duty Montgomery GI Bill and then transferred to a reserve unit may be eligible to have an additional 12 months of reserve GI Bill status on top of the active duty GI Bill they already used. This enables the SCS additional time to use their GI Bill benefits beyond the original 36 months. Likewise, this would be the case for a Reservist who did the opposite (switching to the reserves); ***Note: The maximum payout for the GI Bill combined between reserve and active service is 48 months.***

- As mentioned previously, military members who served on active duty after September 11, 2001 for the aforementioned periods, are eligible for either the post-9/11 GI Bill or Chapter 1606 benefits, whichever they choose;

- If an SCS is an active military member who started using his traditional Montgomery GI Bill benefits, he may switch to the post-9/11 GI Bill benefits if he chooses to do so. However, he must be on active duty for a certain amount of time afterward, and can only switch once;

- Students who used up their 10-year post-service status to use the traditional Montgomery GI Bill, but now qualify for the new post-9/11 GI Bill, may now be eligible to receive education benefits again. For example, if a service member is over the 10-year limit to use his traditional Montgomery GI Bill benefits, but qualifies for the post-9/11 GI Bill, he may be eligible to now receive those benefits due to the increase in time from 10 to 15 years to use the post-9/11 GI Bill. This could apply to a reserve or active veteran.

To determine if you are able to change your GI Bill chapter, please contact the Veterans Administration at the following online link: www.gibill.va.gov/GI_Bill_Info/benefits.htm

Transferring Your GI Bill Benefits To Beneficiaries

For service members still on active duty who have already used a considerable amount of their benefits towards their education and have achieved a level they are pleased with, they can choose to transfer their GI Bill benefits to their dependents. This makes it especially unique among the benefits for education available to the service and makes it a true investment in your education. There are some important things to note here, primarily that not every service branch is eligible for this benefit. (At the time of publication, the Navy and Marine Corps do not allow this transfer.) Additionally, the service member must still be an active duty member at the time of transferring his benefits in order to change the beneficiary of the GI Bill, and must have a certain amount of service time left. This transfer of benefits can be done for both the Chapter 33 and Chapter 30 versions of the GI Bill.

To determine if you are eligible to transfer your current GI Bill status to a dependent, or would like to use the benefits of the service member in your household, contact the VA through the following link: www.gibill.va.gov/GI_Bill_Info/benefits.htm

Activating the GI Bill

Unlike most of the other programs available, the Department of Veterans' Affairs (and not the Department of Defense) allocates the funds for the GI Bill. With that in mind, the benefits must be applied for first through a website called the Veterans Online Application System (VONAPP). The VONAPP website allows you to apply for your GI Bill benefits for any of the aforementioned chapters by completing one of two application forms:

- *Form 22-1990*—Pertains to all applicants applying for GI Bill benefits for the first time AND if you are applying for benefits under a different chapter. For example, changing from Chapter 1606 to Chapter 33 GI Bill benefits;

- *Form 22-1995*—Pertains to all applicants who are transferring their benefits from one institution to another *without* changing chapters.

When you complete the VONAPP, it is electronically submitted to the VA. You will eventually be sent an eligibility form that should be saved in your records and a copy made to be forwarded to your institution. Some institutions may also require you to forward a copy of your completed 22-1990 or 22-1995, for the purposes of certifying your eligibility by contacting the VA and letting them know that you enrolled in courses with the institution. You can print and save the 22-1990 or 22-1995 after submitting it. The link to the VONAPP website is: www.vabenefits.vba.va.gov/vonapp/main.asp

```
Print
  Department of
  Veterans Affairs
APPLICATION FOR VA EDUCATION BENEFITS

1.) SOCIAL SECURITY NUMBER OF APPLICANT
2.) SEX OF APPLICANT
3.) APPLICANT'S DATE OF BIRTH
4.) NAME (First, Middle Initial, Last)
5.) APPLICANT'S ADDRESS
6A.) APPLICANT'S PRIMARY PHONE NUMBER
6A.) APPLICANT'S SECONDARY PHONE NUMBER

6B. APPLICANT'S E-MAIL ADDRESS
7. DIRECT DEPOSIT


7. DO YOU HAVE A CHECKING OR SAVINGS ACCOUNT?


7. NAME OF FINANCIAL INSTITUTION N/A
7. ACCOUNT NUMBER N/A
7. ROUTING NUMBER N/A
8. Name, address, and phone number of someone who will always know where you can be reached
```

Contact's name	
Contact's address	
Contact's phone	

```
9. EDUCATION BENEFIT BEING APPLIED FOR
```

	Conf.#:	VA Form 22-1990 (VONAPP)
SSN:	Submission Date:	Page 1 of 8

VA FORM 22-1990

Sample 22-1990 Application. *Author*

Title IV Federal Financial Aid

Housed within the U.S. Department of Education, the Federal Financial Aid Office is designed to provide financial resources to eligible students beyond the high school level. The financial aid that is provided to eligible students is in the form of grants, low interest student loans, and Parent or Student Plus loans. As a student, it is important to know what is

THE BIG IDEA! *The GI Bill in any form provides the SCS with a great chance to defray college costs through supplemental payment on its own or to other benefits. Use it to help pay for school and, in some cases, even provide support while you are attending. Use your benefits wisely!*

available to you to assist you in funding your education. Also, remember that not all schools are eligible to provide Title IV federal financial aid, and not all educational programs within a particular school are eligible for federal financial aid.

- **The Federal Pell Grant Program**. This federal program provides grants to students for undergraduate and some post-baccalaureate programs based on the student's need. The amount of the grant is determined based on the data submitted on the Free Application for Federal Student Aid (FAFSA) using a standard formula. The grant can be used at any of the participating Institutions of Higher Education (IHE), but you can only use the grant at one IHE at a time. The benefit of a Pell Grant is that you do not have to pay it back to the federal government. The amount that you receive from the Pell Grant program is determined based on your Estimated Family Contribution (EFC) and your academic status, whether you are a freshman, sophomore, junior, or senior. Also, your status (part-time or full-time student) will determine the amount of your Pell Grant. Even if you will be using your branch of service's FTAP to pay for your college education, you should still complete a FAFSA and find out if you are eligible to receive a Pell Grant, which you can use to pay for other educational expenses.

- **Stafford Student Loans**. Stafford student loans are low interest loans for the student that must be paid back to the lender. However, the repayment of these loans does not begin until six months after you have completed your degree program. The amount of the student loan is determined in the same manner as the Pell Grant program.

- **Parent and Student Plus Loans**. Plus loans are available to eligible parents and students to pay for college costs that may not be covered by a Pell Grant, Stafford Loan, or other governmental financial aid programs. The main difference between the Plus loan and the Stafford loan is that repayment of the loan begins immediately, but may be deferred due to a qualifying reason.

LISTEN UP—IMPORTANT POINT!

To start the Title IV Federal Financial aid process, you will need to go to www.fafsa.ed.gov and there complete the application for an electronic PIN, which will allow you to complete your FAFSA electronically. Once you have applied for your PIN you will be able to complete the actual FAFSA. The ultimate purpose of the FAFSA is to determine your Estimated Family Contribution, or EFC. The EFC is determined from the income data that you will enter. The income data will be based on the previous year's tax income from your federal income tax forms. To complete the FAFSA you will need the FAFSA school code for your school. The school code can be obtained from the financial aid office or from the school's website.

The FAFSA is a free application, and you may be eligible for money you don't have to pay back. Why not apply?

In case you did not catch that the first time, the FAFSA is a *FREE APPLICATION*!

Military College Loan Repayment Program

Most branches of the service will offer a College Loan Repayment Program (CLRP) upon initial enlistment. The terms will vary depending upon which branch of the service you join, whether you are active duty or reserves, and what your military occupation will be. These are offered in varying amounts and frequency for two reasons: first, it is used as an enlistment incentive to help achieve recruiting goals. Second, it allows the military to entice educated professionals to fill highly specialized positions.

If you have already completed school and want to eliminate some debt, this program is ideal for you. If you are considering enlisting in the military after school, you should ask your recruiter about the CLRP. Your only requirement may be to join a highly needed occupation specialty. In addition, active duty personnel must waive their GI Bill benefits in exchange for the CLRP (active duty personnel cannot concurrently use the GI Bill and CLRP). However, it could be a big help in paying off your existing student loan debt.

On the reserve end, because the GI Bill and CLRP payouts aren't quite as robust, enlistees do not have to forfeit their GI Bill in order to use the CLRP. At the time of publication, the payment rates are as follows:

- *Air Force*—Maximum payment authorized is $10,000;

- *Air Force Reserves*—Does not offer a CLRP;

- *Army*—Maximum payment authorized is $65,000. Prior service members are not eligible;

- *Army Reserves*—Maximum payment authorized is $20,000 (includes Army National Guard and Air National Guard);

- *Coast Guard*—Does not offer a CLRP;

- *Marine Corps*—Does not offer a CLRP;

- *Navy*—Maximum payment authorized is $65,000. Prior service members are not eligible;

- *Navy Reserves*—Maximum payment authorized is $65,000.

Remember that the amount paid per year and the total package vary greatly under enlistment contracts for each branch of the service. This can be significantly different from the above numbers, and those amounts listed are only maximum payouts. Payments broken down on a year-to-year amount may also change these numbers.

Note: While these CLRP incentives are frequently offered, they are by no means guaranteed. In fact, they can change at any given time without notice, so be careful to make sure you check your contract carefully.

Scholarships

Scholarships are typically merit-based forms of payment for education. The good thing about being an SCS is that there are several scholarships available to you. What's more, while the majority of scholarships are predominantly based on the student's academic ability, scholarships for SCS are often geared towards their connection to the service or career path choices and may not require a certain GPA to apply.

Here are some examples of popular military-specific scholarships:

ROTC Scholarships—Awarded in two-, three-, and four-year designations, these scholarships typically offer a bachelor's degree free of charge or specific dollar amount contributions in exchange for service after graduation as a commissioned officer in the branch of service of the student's choice based on availability.

Intrepid Fallen Heroes Scholarship Fund—Given to recipients whose parent lost his or her life during Operation Iraqi Freedom and Operation Enduring Freedom.

Tillman Military Scholarship—Named in honor of Pat Tillman, former NFL star who was killed in action in Afghanistan after enlisting in the Army. Open to military members and their dependents who are seeking to obtain their education with a goal of positive social change.

Disabled War Veteran Scholarship—$2,500 scholarships available to students who were wounded or disabled during Operation Iraqi Freedom and Operation Enduring Freedom and are pursuing education in specified technical fields.

In addition to these programs, there are hundreds, and perhaps thousands, of regional and local scholarships available to all types of SCS—from active military members to veterans to dependents. Fortunately, there are several search engines available that consolidate these scholarships based on the information provided by the prospective recipient. Here are some websites that our students have had the most success with:

Military.com Scholarship Finder:
http://aid.military.com/scholarship/search-for-scholarships.do;jsessionid=BDF74688E38268C4C3FAOBAF540A63C5

Military Scholar.com Scholarship Finder:
www.militaryscholar.org

Remember that scholarships are *free money* that you do not have to return. It may take a long time to skim through the vast number of scholarships available and apply for each one that is right for you, but the time spent may well put dollars in your pocket that can be allocated toward completing your education.

Benefits Options for Spouses

The recent influx of services geared toward military spouses is a direct reflection of two significant changes happening in military households as of late:

- Military spouses are choosing to join the workforce more so than ever before. The availability of opportunities and the erosion of the household structure with one breadwinner due to economic and social changes have made this a frequent occurrence.

- The increase in duration and frequency of deployments in the new millennium often leave military spouses separated for significant periods of time. Education and to help support the family back home in preparation for future deployments or

THE BIG IDEA! It's no secret that it's hard work trying to find out information about scholarships and applying for them. But the reward of free money to use for your education will outweigh the work you put into it!

the desire to help "pass the time" are often reasons that more and more spouses are seeking education benefits.

This change has left two significant programs created to help spouses obtain education benefits: tuition assistance for spouses through each branch of the service, and Career Advancement Accounts for military spouses.

The spouse tuition assistance programs are available for each branch of the service, in varying capacities, except for the Coast Guard. For the majority of the branches, they are available only for spouses of active service members who are serving overseas. However, for the Army, there is a stateside version available as well.

Here is what is available for each service branch:

- Air Force Spouse Tuition Assistance Program (STAP);

- Army Overseas Spouse Assistance Program (OSEAP);

- Army Stateside Spouse Education Assistance Program (SEAP);

- Marine Corps and Navy Spouse Tuition Aid Program (STAP)

Keep in mind that each service branch has its own terms, payment structures, and availability for which it offers these benefits, and these are *only offered to active duty spouses*. To find out if you qualify or what the benefit for your specific spouse TA plan is, please contact your local ESO.

A Career Advancement Account (CAA) is similar to the spouse TA plan in payment and availability. However, because CAAs are funded by the Department of Labor and Department of Defense, they focus on helping spouses who are at home or abroad, particularly those who transfer between duty stations frequently.

CAAs can be used for many endeavors, ranging from continuing education classes to classes toward a doctorate degree. CAAs will pay for any tuition, training programs, and licensing or certificate fees, but will not pay for things like applications or graduation fees. CAAs are available for active duty military members and deployed members of the reserves, to include the National Guard provided it is for a federal activation, and up to 180 days after the end of the deployment.

To determine your eligibility and apply for a CAA, please go to the following link: https://aiportal.acc.af.mil/mycaa

Veterans

Veterans represent a revered part of the population. The first education benefits were geared specifically toward them as they returned home from World War II, and, within a certain period of time after leaving the service, they may still have access to their GI Bill benefits, along with a wealth of scholarships and other options.

Additionally, to honor our nation's veterans, several states have set up programs where service veterans are able to go to school for a reduced rate. In addition to this, as of the publication date of this book there are six states that offer <u>free</u> <u>tuition</u> for veterans:

Connecticut
Illinois
Montana
Texas
Wisconsin
Wyoming

As a reminder, these tuition waivers are only available for *public* schools within those states. For example, in Connecticut, this waiver is

THE BIG IDEA! *The role of the military spouse is one that cannot be understated. The military has recognized this and made programs available for them. Finding out if you are eligible is up to you.*

available at the University of Connecticut, but not at a private university such as Yale. Keep in mind these states have different requirements (such as residency and duration of service period) and some cover strictly tuition, while others cover other associated fees. Be sure to check the state's ESO listed in the National Guard section for details.

Veterans or Dependents With No Benefits—No Problem!

Despite the wealth of programs available to service members and families, some of you who have purchased this book in the hope of easily finding the holy grail of military benefits available to you, turning page after page in search of it, may be disappointed. This may be because:

- You do not qualify for any of the benefits we've listed here;

- Your benefits have run out.

If this is the case for you, fear not—we may still be able to help you. Keep reading for a couple areas that are worth a try.

If you're a qualified veteran who lives in close proximity to a state with the veteran's benefits we've listed, consider transferring there or, if possible, moving to a state that offers such benefits.

Whatever you do, check out those scholarships mentioned earlier. This will take a considerable amount of time, but the wonders of internet searches now allow you to scan eligible scholarships, stipends, and grants with any number of search engines. Who knows—you just might qualify for one of them!

The last option we're going to mention is to search for schools that offer "military discounts." This is typically geared toward the military student population and can also offer other SCS with no benefit options—older veterans and ineligible spouses and dependents—an opportunity to attend any number of institutions at a discounted price.

The majority of these schools feature distance learning or online programs that can cater specifically to the hectic lifestyle of active duty military and other SCS, and therefore have tailored specific plans to reflect that desired student population. Many of these schools also recognize that the military offers its own unique network of referral opportunities for potential students, and therefore make their programs eligible for any SCS—to include those aforementioned who no longer are eligible for any benefits. What that means for you is a significantly discounted education that can save you a lot of money over a traditional student.

Many of these schools will feature a section on their webpage specifically geared towards the SCS and feature tuitions that make it easy to apply TA and other education benefits to. Some of these schools will even offer other perks such as free books and no student fees to further help defray the cost of education.

> Example: Chris W. was a student at a traditional university. His fears of the burden of increased tuition costs and loan repayments led him to consider other options. Being the son of a Vietnam War veteran, Chris was eligible for a discount at another institution. This saved him a significant amount of money in tuition and, because books were included in the cost, added even more savings. What's more, Chris was pursuing a degree in business but had hoped to begin his own web design venture. With the added flexibility of online classes, Chris is now able to pursue his education at a more affordable rate *and* at a schedule that is flexible to his needs.

ATTENTION: All Tuition Assistance programs, VA Educational Benefits, and other Title IV Federal Financial Aid programs require that you, the SCS, <u>must</u> maintain what is called Satisfactory Academic Progress or "SAP" in order to continue to receive benefits. SAP is determined by your Cumulative Grade Point Average or CGPA. Minimum SAP for the programs mentioned in this book is a 2.0 CGPA—or a C average (based on a 4.0 scale).

THE BIG IDEA! *Whether you are eligible for any military benefits provided by the government or not, as an SCS you can be assured that there is some discount, scholarship, or grant available to you that will recognize who you are and what you've done for this great country!*

CHAPTER 7

What Can I Expect as a College Student?

"A good battle plan that you act on today can be better than a perfect one tomorrow."

— Gen. George S. Patton

What Can I Expect?

For some of you reading this book, this is going to be your first experience in college. So the big question on a lot of your minds is probably, "What can I expect?"

The last time you likely recall asking that question was before you shipped to basic training. Back then, you were probably hoping for a magic answer that was going to be the key to enlightenment and help make the situation as easy as possible. By the time you arrived, however, you quickly realized two things:

1) Everyone you asked gave you a different answer, and . . .

2) Everyone who answered your questions gave you an answer that was based on *their* experience!

The same holds true for the college experience. We can't tell you exactly what to expect from college because there are so many different experiences you may have. The best way, then, to answer your question is to point you in the right direction and help you confront some concerns and thoughts you may (or likely will) have.

If you attend a traditional college classroom as a full-time student or have a schedule that permits you to do so during the day, you will notice a completely different environment and experience than your military experiences. Trust us—it will take some time to get used to this different world of academia. A quick scan in any direction will reveal wide variations in dress, action, speaking, and behavior. You'll see interesting hairstyles, wild clothing choices, and much more. In the classroom, you will discover that students tend to come and go as they please—some shuffling in late with others leaving before the class officially ends. Most professors don't take attendance. They typically run the classroom fairly democratically, and you may hear a lecture interrupted by a student with a question. This all seems obvious, even without attending college, but the shock of transitioning from active-duty military to college is a common issue we hear.

So trust us, all of this will seem pretty unusual if you're coming into a college classroom for the first time after serving in the military. Keep in mind that many "civilian" students will view you as being "different," as well. Younger students in particular may be seeing a military person for the first time. Be aware of that and that there may be a myriad of different reactions to you that you might encounter. If you have to wear your uniform to class because of your schedule, you may find that some students will be intimidated by your dress. Some may stare at you because you are different. You may also notice that students are curious about you and may actually be more apt to strike up a conversation. Some may wonder what you do while others might mention that they have a relative who is also in the service. Even if you don't wear a uniform or even for some veterans who recently left the service, keep in mind that simple things like your haircut, the way you talk in class, or even the way you walk can clue someone in that you are or were a member of the military.

Here is something else to consider: On college campuses, differing opinions and ideologies are encouraged. You may encounter a student who doesn't agree with the principles of the military and may voice his or her opinions to you. Just accept it. After all, you either have or are defending their right to speak out!

LISTEN UP—IMPORTANT POINT!

Regardless of which of the above reactions you receive from other students, do not take anything personally or try to be confrontational. Always respond politely, be courteous, and remember that you are representing the U.S. military. Be friendly, be proud and, if possible, be helpful to your fellow students, and the overwhelming majority of them will have your respect and admiration.

If you are in a distance learning/online or professional program, the chances are you may encounter a population that is predominantly made up of older students. You may find that as an SCS, you are considered a sage who has experienced many things in the military and/or on the battlefield well beyond that of the typical traditional student. Some students may direct questions to you based on your experience and look to you as a source of information based on that experience. You may also encounter some of the same curiosities from students as above. Again, this is perfectly normal.

If you are attending college in the traditional mode (campus-based), spend time on campus and not just when you are there for your classes. Get involved in your campus and the programs it has to offer. You will often notice that there are a seemingly endless number of events you can attend as a student. Enjoy as many of them as possible! If something interests you, become part of it.

For example, you may notice something on campus you'd like to see changed. Attend student government meetings or run for office. There are organizations and clubs on campus for a wide variety of interests, hobbies, and causes. If you enjoy sports, why not attend a game at your school? The homecoming events typically happen in October and can be a great time to show your school pride. Sporting events at some schools, particularly football and basketball, are huge events rivaling professional sports. Games are played in stadiums and arenas often holding tens of thousands of screaming fans and sometimes boast a national television audience. There are also opportunities to see professional quality theater, dance, and music events. Some schools may have spring break activities in April or May before finals that feature live entertainment from big-name artists. Students are often let into these events for bargain prices. Virtually every school has a student center that serves as the hub of campus activities. Events are typically posted or occur there throughout the year. There are also convenience stores (sometimes part of the bookstore) and places to eat and relax on campuses. Campus life can provide a unique respite from the rigors of studying.

__THE BIG IDEA!__ If you live in close proximity to your college, make an effort to become part of the community. Even if you aren't, use your opportunity to meet others and explore life within the student populations of your university!

The Classroom as an Opportunity to Network

One of the facets of education that is often ignored is the opportunity for networking within the classroom and how that can prepare you for your life <u>after</u> your degree. Whether you choose to stay in the military or decide to use your degree or certification to help you in the civilian sector, remember to utilize your classroom time to your benefit. The way to maximize this is to utilize one of the buzzwords of the job market today: <u>networking</u>.

Networking within the classroom is a terrific opportunity for you to expand your circle of people you can look to for advice, guidance, assistance, friendship, and future employment. Networking creates opportunities where none existed before, and can help you turn a good potential opportunity into an incredible real one.

The phenomenon of networking is something that, in the military, you may be quite familiar with. For example, let's say you attended a senior leadership school and kept in contact with one of your classmates who was previously attached to a support operations group. During a discussion, you mentioned you would love to transfer to a support operations group someday. Six months later, you receive an email from that same classmate who let you know that a position opened up in your job description. That's how an ideal networking situation may work within the military.

The principle is the same in the civilian world. The main thing you may experience that is different may depend on your rank. Often, professors at the university you are attending will be far more approachable than those at a military school. Other than that, you have the same scenarios for those who are in class with you: A wealth of people from different walks of life and, depending upon what kind of a program you are in, perhaps from different areas of the country or even the world. Think about how many classes you will have to take before you obtain your degree or certificate. Consider how many professors you will have, and then ponder the large number of students you will see, talk with, and attend class with. Each time you start a new class, a fresh opportunity for networking awaits.

Here are some ways that networking within the classroom can benefit you:

- **Provide you with an opportunity to relate to people in the civilian sector.** Let's face it, for those of you on active duty, military life does not provide much opportunity for civilian interaction. Depending on your job and location, it can be quite limited. Having interaction with students and professors will help you communicate with civilians better and have a better understanding of what you may expect in the workforce once you leave the service.

- **Maintain lasting relationships with people who can help you further your career.** Never downplay the opportunity to network with people in your class. The next person you network with could be the one who helps you with changing your career path or furthering the one you are on!

- **Provide you with an instant support group for your studies.** Remember your battle buddy from basic training? The concept can be the same in the classroom. There's nothing that says you have to work alone. This is the most immediate benefit of networking for the SCS, particularly if you haven't been in a class in awhile or are new to the experience. The student(s) you network with can assist you with getting used to the campus, help with studies, or offer support with empathy and assistance when things get tough.

The great thing about networking is that it is not indigenous to any one specific type of classroom. It works just as well with undergraduate students in 100 level courses as it does with law school students. It works nearly as well in a traditional classroom as it does in an online classroom. Regardless of the forum or the curriculum within your classroom, networking can easily be accomplished and can be a great tool to help you succeed in class—and maybe reach your career goals as well.

Ok, so by now you are sold on the value of active networking. Now you are wondering, "How do I do it within a classroom?" Here are some basic steps that will help you get started and work well with either professors or students:

- **Introduce yourself.** Give more than just your name! Be sure to give enough information to interest people who may want to engage in further conversation. If it's not obvious, tell them you're in (or were in) the military.

- **Reciprocate.** Be equally receptive to people who approach you, and show interest in their background. Answer their questions: civilians will have a natural curiosity in what you do. Ask questions about them to show interest in their lives as well. Networking isn't a one-way street. You may even help someone who is interested in joining the military themselves!

  * Note: Keep in mind that civilians may not be privy to OPSEC. If they pry too far, don't be confrontational and don't withdraw. Explain the circumstances politely and move on.

- **Use your interactions outside of class, or a discussion in class, to get in contact outside the classroom.** Exchange contact information, walk from class together discussing the topic, or head to the campus library and study. This will help forge a bond <u>outside</u> the classroom and establish the networking relationship.

- **Continue to work with the person.** Whether they are instructors or students, interact with them as much as needed during class. Don't let the warm introduction go stale. Students, in particular, can gravitate toward others in a hurry if you let things get stagnant. Don't find yourself on the outside of groups of friends.

- **Maintain relationships.** Once class is over, if you have a classmate or classmates you conversed with or worked with throughout and you feel so inclined, by all means keep in touch. You can utilize instant messaging services, social networking sites such as Facebook, or professional sites such as LinkedIn. If you don't have an account with one of these programs, you should. It's a great way to network and keep in touch with your classmates now and in the future.

- **Keep in touch with your professor (if class went well).** Remember, your professor comes not only with the guidance to help you succeed in the course, but he or she also comes with a background that is reflective of his knowledge and experience to boot. He can play a key role in jump-starting your next career move. Of course he has the education, but imagine the vast number of key contacts he may have who can help you land your next big job. For those of you who are still in the service and don't intend on getting out for some time, don't discount this relationship with your professor. Full-time professors are often fixtures (for decades) at the same institution, or at least within academia in general and are easy to track down. Additionally, if you are considering graduate studies, a former professor's guidance, advice, and letter of recommendation will be invaluable down the road and may provide the weight needed to gain what you need.

Here's one more important thing to consider: utilizing the classroom to get to know others can also a great way for you to gain perspective on people. Relating to people is a big part of the job of senior leadership in the military. As people in the service move up in the ranks, they tend to be more homogenized. They act and think far more alike than those who are new to the service who have not yet gone through an entire career of the military lifestyle. With that in mind, networking within the classroom can help those of you who are senior leaders or aspire to do so to relate to people of varying backgrounds. Classrooms tend to be melting pots of students. This can be helpful in your leadership endeavors.

***THE BIG IDEA!** Networking can provide you an excellent resource towards helping you complete your degree. Your opportunities to meet other people will come in handy and may offer you the support you need for success!*

However networking within the classroom will benefit you, make sure it is part of your plans for school and something you utilize as a tool for your success now and well into the future.

Ensuring Success as an SCS

No one can guarantee you success. You are ultimately responsible for your success in the military and in the workplace, and you will ultimately be responsible for your success in school. There are five important steps you can take to help ensure that you will have every opportunity to achieve success in school.

1. **Make sure you attend or log in to class regularly!** Attending class whenever possible is a mainstay of educational success. It is non-negotiable. Keep in mind that some instructors will have attendance and participation as a percentage of his or her grading. Your failure to regularly attend classes can hurt you.

2. **Keep on top of your course work and try to stay ahead!** The hectic life of a service connected student lends itself to unexpected surprises. It's always best to anticipate these as much as possible and do the work when you have a chance before it affects your schoolwork.

3. **If you have any questions, ASK**! Communication with your instructors and fellow students is key in your success in the class. Interacting with your instructor and fellow classmates will help guide you through this process. If your instructor doesn't have an answer quickly enough, remember that your classmates may be able to help you out.

4. **If you encounter a problem, communicate it with your instructor or advisor IMMEDIATELY**! This cannot be stressed enough and is very important in making sure that you are successful as a student. Notify someone so he or she is aware of any problems that arise. These can include sudden deployments, family emergencies, or drastic increases in

workload. <u>Do not expect a free pass from your instructor because you are in the military</u>! Your instructor does not need to know that you were deployed or extremely busy at work and that's why you didn't show up to class for half of the semester. He wants to know *before* you don't show up for class. There are systems in place to protect military students from academic or financial burdens because of an unavoidable issue. This is understandable. However, in order to put the systems in place, please remember to inform someone as early as possible if you are encountering difficulty in completing your course(s). It's your obligation to keep the lines of communication open. Instructors shouldn't be hunting you down to find out why you have been AWOL to class.

<u>Which leads us to the most important step</u>:

5. **Keep the contact information of your academic advisor with you at all times**. The life of a military member can be chaotic, with events changing at a moment's notice. That's why it's critical to make sure that you have this info at your fingertips. Why? Instructors may come and go throughout your academic career, but your academic advisor will remain with you for most if not all of it. He or she can be a lifeline of communication for you, acting as a liaison who can contact your instructors and let them know of your situation. Keeping her phone number with you at all times is extremely important, because you don't know when you'll have computer access in an emergency call-up or deployment. But you will always have access to a phone. Making that quick call to your advisor should be at the top of your priority list if need be. She can inform your instructors of your situation, help you transition back should the situation be temporary, or help put in place the systems designed to help you return to the school when time and situation permit.

Focus on time management and commit yourself to success and you will achieve this transition in no time. As with any major endeavor in your life, the underlying key to success in your educational pursuits is <u>persistence</u>! Too often we allow the challenges of our jobs, family, and life in general to get in the way of our goal of earning a college credential. The U.S. Census Bureau's 2008 Current Population Survey, Annual Social and Economic Supplement shows that only 22% of the adult population in the U.S above the age of 18 has some sort of a college degree! That is just one in five!

There are many reasons for this in the situation of a Service Connected Student. You may have enlisted into the military right after high school thinking that this was your only way to get ahead. Perhaps you realized that you would not have been able to afford college and the military was a path to being able to afford college later in life. You may not have been a very good student in high school and you didn't think that you would be able to do well in college (and besides, it would be a waste money). You needed to take a break and for you, serving in the military and getting job skills training was the way to do it. Regardless of the reason, as a military student, you now have a tremendous amount of positive things going for you that will help you in your pursuit of your college education.

For one, you now have the financial resources that are needed to pay for a college education that you do not have to repay. You have service based tuition assistance programs and veteran's educational benefits available to you. You are now a little older, more mature, and more confident in your abilities to succeed at anything you set your mind to.

LISTEN UP—IMPORTANT POINT!

Nothing is ever as easy as it seems. As a military student, you will face many more challenges than the traditional college student. Some of them you will have control over; many you will not. You will face deployments to foreign countries and/or war zones. Some of you will be able to plan with advanced notice; many of you will have literally days, and in some cases, just hours to square away your family and your life before you depart. As a military service member, you face the inevitable "Hey sergeant, pack your bags, you're going to the NCO

Academy and you leave tomorrow!" You will have major training exercises that take you away from your life for weeks or months at a time. If you are a member of the National Guard you also face the call to state active duty in the event of a state of emergency due to a natural disaster.

Besides the challenges that military life gives you, you also have the challenge of balancing your family life with the needs of accomplishing the mission when you are not deployed. Military life, let there be no mistake, is stressful, and the last thing that you need to worry about is handing in a homework assignment to some professor who doesn't even know the difference between a T.O.C and a tic-tac!

However, it is just as important to continue your education and to prepare for life after the military as it is to accomplish your military mission. The key is to <u>be persistent</u> in the pursuit of your college education and <u>never</u> lose sight of your goal.

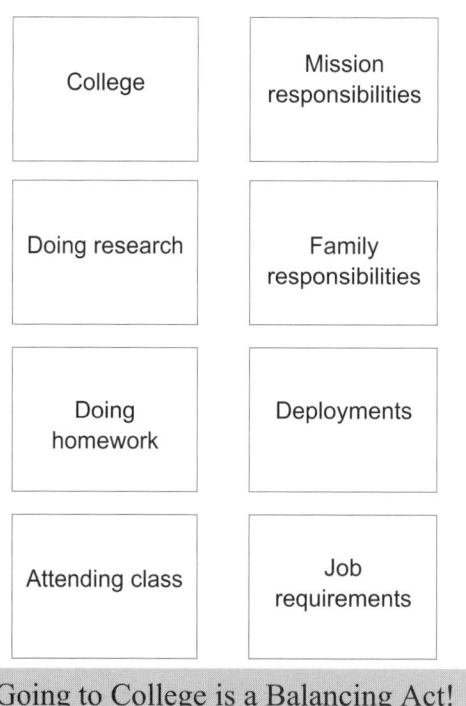

Going to College is a Balancing Act!

Chapter 8

Serving While Studying

"The difference between a successful person and others is
not a lack of strength, not a lack of knowledge,
but rather a lack of will."

— Vince Lombardi

Military Students

This book speaks to many people on many levels, and especially to those Service Connected Students in the middle of their military service, and those of you who are thinking of joining the service (partially to take advantage of education benefits). This does not mean that those of you who are veterans or dependents are not as important, and all of you can use the information in this book to help achieve your educational goals. However, to the broad population learning about the education benefits available to you right now, SCS have the best chance to utilize them.

There are two primary reasons for this. The first is simply that you have more benefits available to you now than in the past. At a minimum, you are able to utilize your Tuition Assistant benefits. As of the release date of this book, the amount of the benefit is $4,500 per year. There are also some important benefits available that you may already have or that can be added on your re-enlistment papers. These "carrots" are there for recruiters to use as tools to get enlistees to join the service, and for students who want to attend a traditional college to earn a bachelor's degree (and are looking to the military for benefits). The wealth of options available include GI Bill "kickers" that enhance the total payout of your GI Bill, in some cases by several hundred dollars per month, or special student loan repayment options. In each of these cases, there is a lot of money available to you to help fund your education for pennies on the dollar, and in some cases go to school at no cost at all.

While these options are important, they may not be the most important reasons that make military education enticing to students who are in the service. Perhaps some of you haven't had an opportunity to consider the military as a career, but this certainly may be a real possibility for you—far more so than you imagined with a civilian education.

Just what can a civilian education do for a member of the military? The truth used to be "not all that much." Often, people joined the service and left after a few years, taking their GI Bill money and Student Loan Repayment plans and trekking to the nearest traditional four-year education. However, times have changed. A civilian education—once considered the domain of officers and a small number of highly-motivated enlisted personnel—is now much more commonplace among the branches of the service. In fact, in some ways military education is now a requirement of the service for anyone seeking any kind of active duty career advancement.

This transition began years ago and coincided with two distinct trends. First, the military has a large hole to fill at the leadership level because in the last decade, thousands of officers have left the service for careers in the corporate sector. The military was slow to realize that, in some respects, it was its own worst enemy when it came to ensuring their officers were well educated. The requirement of officers to hold a bachelor's degree (at a minimum) after a certain period of time made them a coveted asset by the corporate world. While the military can offer a lifestyle of enticing benefits to career officers, it couldn't afford to pay the significant salaries offered by the civilian sector. Thus, for many years most or all of the branches of the service had trouble keeping qualified officers above field-grade rank (major and higher). This trend coincided with the recent expansion of the military (because of the current ongoing wars) and left the military with a huge vacuum at the officer level that needed to be filled.

The second and most important of the two trends is that the military has become highly technical and more thought-oriented in recent years. This, in turn, demands that members of the armed forces be smarter and better trained than ever before. This necessity coincides with the constantly changing and very complex battlefield of today, where the front line has become virtually invisible and reaches well beyond the traditional battlefield. This dramatic change has not only led to the demand for more complex military equipment and procedures requiring a more educated and technically proficient fighting force, but commands the need for more and better educated leaders. Do you want to advance in rank? If so, a civilian education is your best bet.

These two major recent trends have made it especially enticing for the present and future members of the military to obtain their degrees while they are still in the service instead of waiting until their time in the military ends.

LISTEN UP—IMPORTANT POINT!

These trends present a unique and awesome opportunity for those of you who are still considering joining the service or who are still in the early years of your career. The incentive for the military is clear. For those of you who are currently enlisted and want to enhance your education now, consider that this is a clear benefit for you, but also for your branch of the service. Any branch of the military would rather train a capable member of its enlisted ranks to become an advanced leader rather than train an entirely new member of the service. It's in the military's best interest to provide you with that opportunity because you've already proven your worth to the service as a valued asset. This saves the military the cost and the uncertainty of molding a leader from scratch.

If you aren't yet in the service, the opportunity for you is still there to take advantage of utilizing your education to become a leader in the military. You will find that the quicker you accomplish the goal, the faster you become a valuable leadership asset to your peers, and your education may well catapult you up the ranks faster than someone who hasn't yet realized the benefits of obtaining a degree.

More Options, Better Options

Many people reading this book have served their country with honor. Some of you even gained permanent veteran status having served active duty or on a deployment for at least 90 days, while many of you have retired after serving 20 or more years. If you are or were one of these people, chances are you left the service because you were ready to start the next chapter of your life. The fact that you've decided to include education in that next step is a wonderful thing, and your time in service to your country is greatly appreciated. The chances are that you left the service without the education you desired, knowing you would work on getting it when you left. So . . . now is the perfect time.

For those of you who haven't left the service yet and intend on staying in for more than a few years, it's time to discuss what education can do for you while you are still in the military. Some of you may not have considered this before you read this book. The good news is that you've picked an ideal time to at least give it <u>serious</u> thought. Whether you're an E-7 pay grade with five years left until retirement, or an E-3 pay grade who hasn't even thought about re-enlisting (much less retirement), improving your education <u>now</u> (or as soon as possible) will benefit your military career in the long run.

There are a few key ideas that we would like to offer to those of you still on active duty or reserve duty who have not progressed with your civilian education up to this point:

- It's never too early!

- It's never too late!

- It pays to get your degree while you are still in the service!

Chances are you've come up with many reasons to avoid considering school. The two paygrade examples have different reasons to pursue their education. The Senior NCO (E-7) in the above example may have a legitimate gripe about his or her ability to study while serving. Every day military admissions counselors (like us) encounter Senior NCOs who have such heavy workloads that they don't have the time to go to school now. This does not mean you should ditch the idea of going to school. If your workload is really too much to assure success at school, we suggest talking to your commander about your career plans during your next NCOER or review. Demonstrate to your commander how your degree can help you become a more <u>efficient</u> leader of your soldiers, sailors, airmen, or marines, and make you a more <u>effective</u> leader. Communicate your desire to avoid stagnation and ability to reach higher levels. None of this can hurt your cause and often it helps it.

And remember this: The vast majority of commanders <u>want</u> to keep you happy. You're too valuable an asset to him or her as an experienced serviceman, communicator, and provider for the lower-enlisted ranks. Put a bug in your commander's ear about these issues. He or she may be able to delegate some of your workload to others to help you achieve your goals for the overall good of the service. You may even find that your commander will be willing to give you extra time to study and prepare assignments to ensure your success.

However, if you are the junior soldier in the above example (E-3 grade), what's keeping you from going to school? Time off is usually more plentiful for lower-enlisted ranks, as are responsibilities. So we ask you again . . . Why are you not seeking an education?

You may be thinking that you will leave the service in a few short years and then pursue your education. Or, you may think that now is not the right time (for a variety of reasons), and that waiting until you retire or until you have a few more years under your belt makes more sense. If so, you need to consider this question: What makes you think you are going to have an easier time in school five years from now? You will have more responsibilities as a leader by then, and thus won't have the time you may have now. Additionally, your lifestyle may (and almost certainly will) change. You may also have a family, or may change your mind about staying in until retirement and leave without taking full advantage of your benefits.

The bottom line is simple: The sooner you take advantage of your benefits, the better the chance you will get the most out of them. Here are a few reasons why:

- **More money available to you!** The sooner you use your benefits, the more opportunity you'll have to use incentives available to you while you stay in the service (Federal Tuition Assistance, for one example). This will allow you to allocate more funds toward your college education in the long run and allowing other benefits, such as your GI Bill, to last longer.

- **The ability to choose your career path!** The chances are you will open up many doors for yourself with a degree in hand, many you had never considered. It may allow you to get a private sector career opportunity, or more opportunities for advancement while you are still in the service. Which leads us to the next reason . . .

- **Promotion potential!** This speaks solely to the military front. The military would love nothing more than to have a highly educated fighting force as we mentioned previously. While it may not be immediately evident how much this can benefit you from your current status, the next section will give you an enhanced breakdown of how your degree can help you.

***THE BIG IDEA**! By beginning the process of achieving your educational goals now while you are still in the service, you will find the benefits of doing so may be more than you think!*

Progressing Through the Enlisted Ranks

As we mentioned earlier, education is no longer strictly an officer's game. It is in the best interest of the military to have an enlisted force that is better educated than any other fighting force in the world. It is how we gain an advantage on the battlefields of today—and tomorrow. One of the tag lines is that "education will help you maintain and improve the most important weapon of all—your mind."

Think about that for a minute.

Without your ability to think clearly, communicate effectively with others, and perform tasks to their highest level, where would you be? Imagine the advantage you will have over everyone else if your mind is sharper, thinks faster, and makes better and more informed decisions. A degree is often just as good a gauge of how effective you are as a service member as are your military achievements and awards that you proudly display.

Your leaders recognize this and covet your degree by offering you more opportunities for promotion once it is completed. With a degree in hand as soon as possible, you will be able to gain an advantage over many of your counterparts who are competing for those same positions. This is especially important when you realize that many other personnel are seeking promotion to E-5 and E-6. Having that degree in hand will greatly increase your ability to obtain the promotion you desire, and progress through the ranks quickly. Your time at E-5 and E-6 also pass more quickly because you will find yourself eligible for promotion sooner.

LISTEN UP—IMPORTANT POINT!

When climbing the Senior NCO ladder to E-7, E-8, and E-9, having a bachelor's degree in your hip pocket becomes even more important. As you progress up the ranks, you will quickly discover that there are a number of other people who also have several attributes that make them desirable for promotion as well. Some of them may have special skills or qualifications that give them a distinct advantage. The great equalizer, however, is education.

The importance of having a degree has progressed from being "a nice thing for a Senior NCO to have" (20 years ago) to a virtual necessity to achieve that designation in the first place (today). Because the competition is so stiff at the top of the ladder, anything you can do to make yourself stand out with distinction is going to give you an advantage over the competition. Make no mistake: as it stands right now, progressing on to higher enlisted ranks does not require you to have a degree of any sort. However, look around at those who have achieved that rank. Chances are, you will find that many of them do indeed have some college education under their belts.

> *Example:* Mark H. is an active duty Army recruiter from Tennessee. He was interested in furthering his education, but was unable to complete it because of his daily service responsibilities. Finally, Mark found an online program that offered him the flexibility to meet the needs of his hectic military lifestyle and allowed him to attend classes while handling his recruiting duties. Mark's initial goal was to

complete his degree *someday before he got out.* Now, with a renewed desire to complete his degree while he is still early in his career (he is an E-5 with six years of service left), Mark is looking to transition to Officer Candidate School within the next two years.

THE BIG IDEA! *Taking advantage of your education benefits can greatly help you determine which career path you are going to take during your military career—and after. Taking advantage of them now can help you use the most benefits to your advantage.*

Deployed Students

With the influx of troops being added to our military since the start of the wars in the Middle East, deployed military students (once considered an anomaly) have become commonplace. The existence of military students deployed overseas falls into two significant categories you should understand:

- Students who are attending a traditional college, but are temporarily not enrolled due to a military deployment;

- Students who are currently overseas, but attending schools in non-traditional classroom environments—distance learning courses on satellite campuses or online programs.

Each of these categories has some unique challenges associated with deployed students that pertain to each student type. Students who are deployed while attending traditional universities, for example, typically have to leave their colleges and return at a later time. As you can imagine, this raises difficulties and three common questions:

A student study group for overseas online students. *Author*

- Can students return to their institution with their academic standing intact upon return from a deployment? *Yes, you may return with your standing intact following a deployment.*

- Do professors make concessions for classes interrupted by a sudden deployment? *As a rule, your instructors will usually make concessions for any classes interrupted by a sudden deployment. (Students can also petition to have grades reviewed under these circumstances.)*

  * Note: It is incumbent upon you the student to inform the school and provide documentation of your deployment at your earliest available opportunity. <u>Don't assume the school was aware of your circumstances</u>.

- As a current student, can I defer payment on my student loans during deployment? *Yes. Students may defer payment if the deployment is related to a military deployment.*

These measures are put in place to make sure that the SCS attending a traditional college does not have to bear unnecessary burden because a deployment is keeping him or her from attending school.

Students attending school while serving overseas usually do so because these programs offer them the most flexibility (and, betting on their imminent deployment, were right), or were able to take classes toward their degrees at another institution so they wouldn't fall behind on their educational goals. This is, of course, an excellent option.

If this is the case, the SCS has an equally difficult issue to deal with: Attending school at a university while deployed in a combat zone.

Let that sink in for just a minute . . .

Your college campus is not only thousands of miles away, but you have other responsibilities and dangers to deal with that other students do not have to even think about in their day-to-day lives. These can include any of the following:

- **Communication**: Of course, your ability to take courses has a lot hinging on it, namely the need to have a working computer for some courses on-site at the base where you are located, or reliable internet access to do coursework or contact instructors for online courses.

- **Duty First**: This is a pretty basic point. If you're deployed, you can't stop doing your job when you're supposed to just because you have class. And you don't have the benefit of leaving the office!

- **Simulating the Experience**: What about supplies to complete an assignment? Do you have access to them? Or to a quiet place to study? And how about getting books to your location? Sometimes that provides a unique challenge in and of itself.

THE BIG IDEA! *A deployment no longer means putting your education on hold. So long as you have the time and ability, you have many options available to you to continue your education and continue to use your benefits while serving. Be aware that your situation means that you need to plan even better!*

- **Safety**: Going to school under dangerous conditions is no joke and is more common than many people here in the States think. The threat is <u>real</u>, and you may have to be away from class for some time depending upon safety issues.

All these issues (and many more) explain why it is so important to maintain contact with your instructors and advisor regularly, and to take advantage of your downtime to work on your education. Don't assume that your day off on Friday will be your day off.

In light of the struggles of taking classes in a combat zone, if you approach it correctly and make sure you allow yourself ample time and opportunity for success, this is a great way to jump-start your education. If you are searching for motivation, consider where you are and what you are doing for your country. If that doesn't motivate you to take advantage of classes, nothing will!

For those SCS who currently attend a traditional school but find some downtime during a deployment, taking courses online and at a satellite campus on a base (many schools feature such options) are also great ways to continue your education while you are gone.

NOTE: For those of you attending traditional universities who wish to take online courses that will allow you to continue pursuing your degree while you are deployed, be sure to verify <u>with your academic advisor at your home school</u> whether those courses will transfer!

The message here is clear: If you have time and your duty allows, taking courses while deployed is an excellent way to continue—or start—your education. Here is another real-life example:

> Anika A., a student deployed in Iraq, signed up for courses at an online school before she left to go overseas. As an Army reservist, Anika does her class work during the week on her off-time away from her duties as an administrative specialist. Not only has she managed to successfully juggle her education while deployed, but she also joined with other students in her unit taking classes. They formed study groups, since some of them are in the same classes at the same school. Doing her class work during her "free time" has also helped her deployment move along quicker, all while achieving one of her goals of starting her education and working toward a degree!

Becoming an Officer

Maybe it's something you've never considered or something you scoffed at in the past. Remaining an enlisted military person for someone who loves what they do is a wonderful career move, and you will certainly find that your degree will enhance and reward your career. But becoming an officer may be a logical step for advancing your career in the military and taking full advantage of the service and obtaining your degree.

The benefits to becoming an officer are better pay, new challenges in leadership and decision-making, and an increased opportunity to put your degree to use in the service. There are several paths to becoming an officer that you can utilize through furthering your education.

Officer Candidate School

As a member of the military, branches have a direct source for creating officers: Officer Candidate School (referred to as Officer Training School in the Air Force). This usually consists of distinct phases involving training to become an officer and skills within the branch of certification.

The seeds of Officer Candidate School (or OCS) were planted in the late 1800s as a selection service to find the best and brightest military leaders. Prior to World War II in the mid-1930s, in anticipation of the need for more officers to field a larger military force as hostilities erupted around the world, the United States Army created a plan to create a school to specifically train officers. These schools were initially divided on several bases throughout the country, but were eventually streamlined in the latter part of the Vietnam War as the draft came to an end. Today, OCS for the various branches exists in locations at the heart of their training areas and, particularly in the Army and Navy, newly commissioned officers are then sent to areas to participate in field-specific training.

THE BIG IDEA! Officer Candidate School can be a great way to enhance your career in many ways. Using your educational benefits gives you the qualifications necessary to apply!

The requirements for OCS vary from branch to branch as far as the battery of tests needed to qualify, and certain requirements for service commitment after commissioning. A person who is entering the standard OCS program is a prior military enlisted member and has attended basic training within his or her respective branch of the service. Some branches also have waivers on age and rank, but typically you should expect to be under 35 years old and with a pay grade no higher than an E-7 in order to be considered for OCS.

Qualifications for each branch of the service vary for education requirements as well. Typically, you need to earn 90 college credits before starting OCS. Obtaining the 90 credits is the difficult part for many individuals, which is where working on your college education as early in your enlistment as possible will garner you benefits down the road. Though you were previously a capable member in good standing in the military, you will not be considered deployable while serving in OCS, and your soul focus will be on your training. After completing OCS and becoming commissioned, you will have one year to complete your bachelor's degree (120 credits). If you are starting with zero college credits and are a junior enlisted soldier, it's recommended you find a program that will get you to an associate's degree (60 credits) the fastest, and then begin pursuing your bachelor's degree to make up the other credits to allow you to progress toward OCS. The reason this is the best path to meet the OCS requirement is that you may have a better chance of being promoted to the next rank with an associate's degree under your belt. The additional experience as an enlisted military member will help you compete with the others applying for those same OCS slots and will make you a more effective leader when the time comes for your commissioning. Remember: once you are commissioned, *it is critical that you obtain your remaining 30 credits within a year to meet your commissioning requirements*! Be especially mindful of this. Waivers may be granted for deployments, but try to get it out of the way as soon as possible and allow yourself the maximum opportunity to complete your degree.

If you haven't yet entered the service and are interested in participating in OCS, you will need to complete initial basic training with your service branch before attending your respective branch's OCS training program. OCS is available as a commissioning route for new enlistees who have already obtained their college degrees *prior* to enlisting and have signed up for OCS as part of their enlistment contract.

Reserve Officer Training Corps

Those of you who are currently enlisted and are below the age of 24 with no college credits, or not older than 25 with sophomore status, may want to consider Reserve Officer Training Corps (ROTC) as a gateway to commissioning. This is an ideal choice if you have no military experience and are coming out of high school, or are currently in your freshman or sophomore year in college.

The roots of Reserve Officer Training Corps sprouted in 1819 at Norwich University in Vermont. There, Captain Alden Partridge, an army officer and former West Point instructor, wanted to incorporate a broader academic sampling at his school than he believed was being taught at West Point. Eventually, this model was used by several universities later in the 1800s as the Morrill Land-Grant Colleges Act, which was signed by Abraham Lincoln. This act allowed states to receive a grant of land to be used for colleges provided they offered some form of military training. Many of these schools would feature military training programs similar to the one enacted by Capt. Partridge at Norwich, which in turn transformed into the ROTC programs that are relatively commonplace in higher education today. When the view toward military presence on college campuses turned negative during the 1960s, some prominent schools eliminated the ROTC training programs. The renewed interest and appreciation for our military in the 21st Century has begun reversing this trend, and several institutions are adding ROTC as they grow to help spur continued growth and student population diversity.

This trend allows those of you who are still in your early twenties and reading this book a remarkable opportunity to become an officer as a reservist <u>while</u> obtaining your college education. ROTC, in conjunction with satellite training battalions on larger college campuses throughout the country, is present in almost every region throughout the United States and its territories. Many larger state and private schools offer ROTC training for cadets directly on their campuses, but several others offer ROTC training on other college campuses nearby through an agreement with another institution. Therefore, even if a college local to you doesn't have its own ROTC training battalion, you can still participate in an ROTC program with that school. ROTC programs available for each branch of the service vary in availability state to state, with the Army ROTC program being available in the most locations because it is the largest branch of the service.

LISTEN UP—IMPORTANT POINT!

ROTC offers two opportunities for college students: An ROTC scholarship, whereby the student's education is usually paid for in full, and ROTC training concurrent with their college education, where the student may not have a scholarship, but will receive reserve pay commensurate with the rates for the ROTC cadets for their service branch. Both programs give students an opportunity to become a commissioned officer of their respective service branch when they receive their bachelor's degrees.

Unlike OCS, which requires completing most of your education on the front-end of qualifying to become an officer, ROTC does not have any such requirements. ROTC scholarship payouts vary with each branch of the service, but they typically offer some combination of the following:

- **Duration of scholarship anywhere from 2-4 years**: This depends on the student's status in school. If they are still in high school or haven't yet attended college, they could apply for a 4-year scholarship. If they are a sophomore or freshmen, they may be eligible for a 2-3 year scholarship, depending on time left until earning their bachelor's degree;

- **100% Tuition, or a flat per-year dollar amount**: This may also be awarded for payment for in-state school tuition fees only;

- **Additional funding/stipend for books**: This is very helpful, as college text books are very expensive;

- **Pay for reserve training periods**: Commensurate with pay grades and sign-up bonuses available for each branch of the service.

Students who are prior enlisted service members can also receive ROTC scholarships, provided certain qualifications are met. These vary, but may include a written letter of recommendation from the unit commander, and a minimum college GPA of at least 2.5. Participation in ROTC at a university for an active enlisted member of the military means that his status temporarily changes to reserve while completing his degrees and he returns to active duty upon commissioning.

To maintain your ROTC scholarship, you need to maintain a consistent GPA (typically above a 2.5) throughout your commission. Failure to do so could result in any number of outcomes, from having to return the scholarship money to enlisting in the service. *Keep in mind that the scholarship carries a service requirement after completion.*

Non-scholarship ROTC programs are also available depending upon the service branch. In the Army, this is referred to as the "Green To Gold" program. Those who participate in Green To Gold or similar programs within other service branches typically receive the reserve monthly training pay for the authorized pay grade, but may also receive additional stipends. These are ideal for those who have prior service credentials in the military, but may not have the academic background to be eligible for a scholarship. Benefits such as the GI Bill can be used to bridge the gap to help pay tuition and other costs associated with college.

ROTC is an outstanding program for a number of reasons. It is the best combination of college education and military officer training that can be completed early in your military career. Because your military classroom experience is intertwined with your academic courses, it develops a synergy between education and military service that will offer you a remarkable opportunity to fuel your continued education throughout your lifetime. The fact that the program is completed before your twenties are over enables you many years to forge your mark as a leader in the service, and allows you opportunities to progress your education further to advanced graduate and professional degrees and certifications. Additionally, ROTC offers some unique training opportunities in areas that you may not normally be able to obtain. These can include specialized schools such as ranger and airborne training, as well as flight school. As with OCS, you are <u>not</u> capable of deploying while in ROTC. Additionally, you are <u>not</u> serving in the capacity of a commissioned officer until graduation.

If you would like further information on ROTC offerings in colleges in your area, please go to the following websites:

Air Force:
www.afrotc.com

Army:
www.goarmy.com/rotc

Navy/Marines:
www.nrotc.navy.mil/

Coast Guard: As of the date of this printing, the Coast Guard does not offer an ROTC program on college campuses.

Service Academies/Military Universities

The service academies for the military graduate commissioned officers to all branches of the service. They are the smallest and most exclusive source of commissioning officers into the United States Military, but are widely considered the education institutions with the longest and steepest military traditions.

The first service academy was the United States Military Academy at West Point, an institution created on a parcel of land that was already steeped in military history. Coveted for its strategic location on the banks of the Hudson River in New York, the land played a major role during the Revolutionary War. The school was built on the grounds in 1802 and since then has served as the model for military academies that followed later in the 19th and 20th centuries. The academic reputations were outstanding from the start. For many decades West Point was widely considered one of the preeminent engineering institutions in the nation. Additionally, the military training programs for its officers were the blueprint for all schools of higher education—including service academies, military universities, and ROTC programs—that have since developed to train our military leaders.

LISTEN UP—IMPORTANT POINT!

There are service academies that train and educate officers for all service branches, complete with commissioning and a bachelor's degree. The education is fully paid for and costs the student nothing. Like ROTC, payment comes in the form of an active duty requirement in the branch of service in which the student was trained. The distinct difference from other routes to obtaining a degree while completing military service is that the military training and discipline is a consistent presence throughout the life of a student. College life here will be extremely different than on a traditional campus, and most of the descriptions of campus life noted elsewhere in this book do not apply. Because all of your classmates are also aspiring military officers, no one attending the service academy is considered a civilian and everyone has to participate in similar training, exercises, and programs.

Although they do not offer graduate-level programs, the academies are known for their unmatched academic and physical rigor and discipline at the undergraduate level. The academies are extremely exclusive, which means the acceptance rate for these schools is extremely low. The requirements for admission typically involve being near or at the top in academic standing in your graduating high school class and a Letter of Nomination from a federal member of Congress (senator or representative), the vice-president, or the president of the United States. Additionally, the applicants must be deemed capable of rigorous military training. Current enlisted members of the military service are eligible to apply for one of the service academies, but must meet the same standards as applicants with no prior military service. Again, you are not considered a commissioned officer and cannot hold the post of one until you graduate with a bachelor's degree from one of these institutions.

Each branch of the service has at least one service academy that trains and educates a percentage of its officers. These academies are as follows:

- **United States Air Force Academy**: Service academy since 1954 located in Colorado Springs, Colorado. Its students are known as Cadets and upon graduation are commissioned Second Lieutenants in the Air Force. www.usafa.af.mil/

- **United States Coast Guard Academy**: Service academy since 1876 located in New London, Connecticut. Its students are known as Cadets and upon graduation are commissioned Ensigns in the Coast Guard. www.cga.edu

- **United States Merchant Marine Academy**: Service academy since 1943 located in Kings Point, New York. Its students are known as Midshipmen. It is the only service academy that trains officers for every branch of the military, though it primarily commissions Ensigns in the Navy. This is also the only academy that offers the option to its students of a non-military obligation after receipt of a bachelor's degree. www.usmma.edu

- **United States Military Academy**: Service academy since 1802, the oldest of the academies and located in West Point, New York. The school's students are called cadets and commissioned Second Lieutenants in the Army after the completion of their bachelor's degree requirements. www.usma.edu

- **United States Naval Academy**: Service academy since 1845. The naval academy is located in Annapolis, Maryland. The students are referred to as midshipmen and are commissioned Ensigns in the Navy or Second Lieutenants in the Marine Corps upon completion of their bachelor's degree requirements. www.usna.edu

In addition to the service academies, there are also military universities. These schools tend to offer a hybrid between the service academies and the traditional ROTC education offered by several institutions. The reason for this is historical in nature: the aforementioned Norwich University is known as the "Birthplace of ROTC" and was where the framework for the merging of a traditional and military education originated.

While similar in curriculum and structure to their service academy brethren, these schools usually offer a less homogenized version of the service academies, with nods to more traditionally-styled schools. This is because military universities are not federal education institutions, but state or privately funded universities. For example, the schools typically feature programs leading to commission in all branches of the service. Most of the schools don't require their graduates to pursue military careers after graduation. Others allow traditional non-cadet students to participate in programs, and the larger schools like Virginia Tech and Texas A&M have a civilian student population that dwarfs that of the military student population. These schools also typically feature comprehensive graduate-level programs available to all students. Think of it as a military college environment on a traditional college campus.

These colleges typically commission a small number of officers per year, and while less selective than the service academies, they are also steeped in some of the same military traditions. The schools considered as military universities include:

North Georgia College and State University
www.ngcsu.edu/

Norwich University
www.norwich.edu/

Texas A&M University
www.tamu.edu/

The Citadel
www.citadel.edu/main/

Virginia Military Institute
www.vmi.edu/

Virginia Polytechnic (Virginia Tech)
www.vt.edu/

THE BIG IDEA! *Becoming an officer offers the active military SCS an incredible opportunity to take their education to the next level, along with their military careers, and arguably offers them the best opportunity to put their education to use.*

Direct Commissioning

Direct commissioning is the most exclusive way to become an officer in the military. The reason for the exclusivity is due to the highly specialized areas and experience and/or advanced degree requirements needed to obtain a direct commission in the service. If you are using this book to help obtain your education, the chances are you are not qualified at this time for a <u>direct</u> commission. However, you can certainly look to obtain one down the road. For example, you may want to earn a degree in a medical field; becoming a nurse or physician's assistant would qualify you as a candidate for direct commissioning. You may also be eligible for commissioning with a related degree in a field such as social work or in a specialty like chemistry or biology, coupled with enlisted leadership experience. The same holds true for becoming a lawyer or a medical doctor. Even with advanced degrees (doctor or lawyer, for example), the entrance rank is typically at the level of O-3 (Captain) in the Army, while the lower-level medical degrees are commissioned as O-1 (Second Lieutenant). Becoming a Chaplain is another route to direct commissioning. These are typically the only three paths to direct commissioning in the Army, and are usually accepted in most of the other service branches as well.

Due to the highly technical aspect of the Navy, Air Force, and Coast Guard, these branches offer some direct commissions for professionals with engineering backgrounds and in fields such as intelligence and public affairs. The Marine Corps, however, does not offer direct commissioning as an option.

Down the road, if your education progresses and you obtain one of the above specialized degrees, contact your commander or local recruiter for more details on how to obtain a direct commission.

Warrant Officer

A Warrant Officer, while not a commissioned officer, is a highly skilled technical position within some branches of the service. Becoming a Warrant Officer involves training for a specific technical duty and entry into Warrant Officer Candidate School (WOCS). Some branches of the service also require that an enlisted person acquire a specific rank before applying for Warrant Officer school. Though a degree is not a requirement, one of the chief prerequisites for most WOCS participants is that they have passed English Composition and English Composition and Literature (usually referred to as ENG 101 and ENG 102). This requirement, coupled with the encouragement to pursue a degree for Warrant Officers, make earning your degree a bonus for those of you who are currently Warrant Officers or are considering taking the step. This is especially important because Warrant Officers are typically used in highly skilled areas such as flight or technician positions. Though all branches of the military have available space for Warrant Officers, the Air Force does not currently have any Warrant Officers. To find out more about becoming a Warrant Officer, please go to the following links:

Army: www.usawocc.army.mil/

Coast Guard: www.cga.edu.ldc_display.aspx?id=652

Marines: www.marines.mil/units/hqmc/pages/default.aspx

Navy: www.ocs.navy.mil/ldo_program_overview.asp

The Active Reserves

Reserve duty status in the military offers a person enlisting for the first time the best opportunity at achieving his education while serving his country. Similar to the reserve status in the ROTC program, you are only required to drill part of the time. The typical weekend drills (and two-week annual training period) encompass a minimum of 38 days per year. There are also times when flexibility may be offered in drilling periods (such as alternative annual training periods to make room for summer courses, etc.) Like active duty, there are also opportunities for promotion in the enlisted ranks and commissioning in the reserves that will allow you to be rewarded for obtaining your degree(s) as you progress.

However, keep in mind that as an enlisted member of the reserves, *you are still considered a deployable asset to your unit*. In other words, if your unit is going to be activated for a deployment, you will probably be part of that deployment; whereas your status in an officer training program makes you non-deployable. That means that reserve duty status does not guarantee that you will be able to complete your college education without military interruption.

Reservists get similar benefits to their active duty counterparts, but often have different ways of being paid benefits. For example, a reservist is eligible for Federal Tuition Assistance, but receives a GI Bill payment automatically and does not have to sign up for it and pay into it like their active duty counterparts do. The amount is far less, but available immediately. Additionally, reservists have the ability to participate in drills with units close to their schools of choice, which offers them an ability to choose a unit close to their school or their home. This means they don't have to worry about getting shifted to an area where they will be forced to change schools, such as an active duty person who may have to PCS (Permanent Change in Station) to another base. In admissions, the phenomena of military students with multiple transcripts from several

THE BIG IDEA! *Transitioning to reserve status or joining the reserves initially is a great way to move forward with your education if you have the ability to do so. Reservists have the best ability to balance military service with education and—with the ideal opportunity and right circumstances for maintaining your lifestyle. This can help you gain an advantage during and after your time in the classroom!*

schools to evaluate is far less of a problem with reservists who, if transferring from another school, may have only that school's transcripts to evaluate because they don't need to change schools due to change in duty station and can usually stay at the same unit for as long as they want or need to remain.

The military reserves also feature similar opportunities for advancement. Each of them offers the same basic schools and opportunities for advancement in the enlisted ranks and commissioning, though the schools may be more regionalized depending upon the branch of the service. Access to the schooling may or may not also be more exclusive. As a reservist, you can also use this as a gateway to determining if the military is right for you after college. Finding it easier to serve concurrently with education may give you more opportunities when you obtain your degree if you decide to pursue active duty or continue as a reservist.

There are some of you who are currently serving on active duty who, for whatever reason, don't have the opportunity to further your education at this time. Still, you may want to take advantage of your military education benefits while still serving to maximize your opportunities. For example, you may wish to utilize federal tuition assistance. Keep in mind that you may also, at the end of your enlistment on active duty, continue to serve your country in the reserves. It is not uncommon for active duty military personnel to continue to serve their country in the reserves after completing time on active duty. There are even opportunities for serving as a reservist in another branch of the service from which you received training initially without going through their initial basic training course. The only branch of the service that requires you to go through basic training if you wish to transition to that branch from another branch is the Marine Corps.

So, if you still don't have family obligations that require you to remain active, or if you have arrangements that preclude you from having to work full-time to support yourself while serving in the reserves, you have a unique opportunity to continue serving and use benefits while attending school full-time. If you continue as a reservist, your promotions earned will continue to progress as your education does. Transitioning back to active duty upon completing your education may require you to complete a few additional requirements to maintain rank or training qualifications, but typically transfer over without a hitch.

There are reserve branches for each branch of the service. To find out more about joining these branches in initial enlistment or after serving on active duty, follow these links:

Air Force Reserves
www.afreserve.com

Army Reserves
www.usar.army.mil/arweb.pages.default.aspx

Coast Guard Reserves
www.uscg.mil/reserve

Marine Reserves
www.marforres.usmc.mil/

Navy Reserves
www.navyreserve.com

National Guard

Though considered a part of the reserves in its own right, the National Guard deserves its own section. As a force that falls under federal *and* state jurisdictions, the National Guard is eligible for unique benefits that vary greatly state to state.

The National Guard is the oldest fighting force, predating even the formation of our nation. When the original settlers arrived in the early 1600s, a system of protection was needed. It was with this concept in mind that militias were formed and eventually, within the colony of Massachusetts, organized as regiments to protect the settlers. When the United States was born, the militias for each state were similarly formed. In 1916, the National Guard as we know it today was organized and became part of the Regular Army. The formation of the Air Force included adding the Air National Guard to the National Guard's force in 1947. Though primarily used for federal duty and deployments, to include massive deployments of personnel during World War II,

Vietnam, and the current wars in Afghanistan and Iraq, the National Guard has another dimension that makes it inherently different from other branches of the service: Each National Guard belonging to each state or territory may be called up by the governor for emergencies within that jurisdiction in addition to federal call-ups. In recent years, crises within states as diverse as floods and snowstorms bring National Guard troops to assist, including larger-scale disasters and emergencies like Hurricane Katrina. This additional state jurisdiction means that each National Guard, though a federal fighting force under the Air Force or Army control, has differing commands that vary state to state.

So what does this mean to you as a student looking to utilize National Guard benefits at some point in time? The education benefits can vary state to state as well.

For starters, if you are serving as an active member of the National Guard (Active Guard/Reserve), you are given the same benefits that active duty army personnel receive. Your GI Bill, Tuition Assistance, and other benefits operate in pretty much the same manner. However, if you are a reservist, circumstances in this regard can and usually are very different.

Reservists in the National Guard fall under two categories: Active Duty for Special Work (ADSW), which includes those who are on temporary active duty orders or technical positions, and traditional reservists (M-DAY). The reservists have a number of different benefits available to them that vary state to state. These may include Federal Tuitition Assistance, State Tuition Waiver, or State Military Grants. This means that there may be a limit on how many dollars are available for tuition assistance, and how many soldiers or airmen are able to take advantage of them. Additionally, each state as part of the enlistment incentive to its National Guard offers widely varying incentives to its enlistees. These range from enlistment bonuses to reduced or free tuition rates to state universities and community colleges.

In addition to Montgomery GI Bill payment and tuition assistance to schools, along with several other programs such as Student Loan Repayment, offered by other service branches, most states offer (at the very least) a discounted rate of varying percentage or dollar amount toward any number of public institutions within the state. At press time, the following states offer 100% free tuition to their state schools and community colleges as part of their benefits packages upon enlistment into the National Guard:

          Alaska
         Colorado
        Connecticut
        Delaware
         Florida
         Georgia
         Hawaii
         Illinois
         Indiana
         Kansas
        Kentucky
        Louisiana
         Maine
      Massachusetts
     New Hampshire
       New Jersey
       New Mexico
        New York
       North Dakota
         Ohio
        Oklahoma
         Texas
Washington (Free tuition offered at Washington State University exclusively)
       West Virginia
        Wisconsin
        Wyoming

    Coupled with the regular benefits offered to reservists, it's easy to see why the National Guard is a terrific choice for someone looking to obtain their degree inexpensively without having to go on active duty, and with added benefits that the regular reserves cannot match. The flagship schools covered by the above states include some of the finest public institutions of education in the country, and with tuition free and the ability to drill at a unit in close proximity to your school, you can earn your degree at a fraction of the cost of most traditional schools.

    To find out the benefits available within each specific state National Guard unit, you should contact your Education Officer within the state you will be serving in. As of the time of publication of this book, here are the phone numbers for each state ESO:

State Education Services Officers (ESOs) Phone Numbers:

Alabama	(334) 213-7580	Montana	(406) 324-3237
Alaska	(907) 428-6477	Nebraska	(402) 309-7313
Arizona	(602) 267-2885	Nevada	(775) 887-7326
Arkansas	(501) 212-4021	New Hampshire	(603) 227-1550
California	(916) 854-3225	New Jersey	(609) 562-0654
Colorado	(303) 677-8959	New Mexico	(505) 474-1245
Connecticut	(860) 524-4816	New York	(518) 786-6039
Delaware	(302) 326-7044	North Carolina	(919) 664-6272
District of Columbia	(202) 685-9812	North Dakota	(701) 333-3064
Florida	(904) 823-0350	Ohio	(614) 336-7023
Georgia	(404) 675-5302	Oklahoma	(405) 228-5251
Guam	(671) 647-2753	Oregon	(503) 584-3456
Hawaii	(808) 733-4120	Pennsylvania	(717) 861-2717
Idaho	(208) 422-3761	Puerto Rico	(787) 289-1502
Illinois	(217) 761-3782	Rhode Island	(401) 275-4109
Indiana	(317) 964-7017	South Carolina	(803) 806-4253
Iowa	(515) 252-4468	South Dakota	(605) 737-6729
Kansas	(785) 274-1081	Tennessee	(615) 355-3968
Kentucky	(502) 607-1307	Texas	(512) 782-5515
Louisiana	(504) 278-8531	Utah	(801) 523-4537
Maine	(207) 626-4370	Vermont	(802) 338-3348
Maryland	(410) 576-1499	Virgin Islands	(340) 712-7785
Massachusetts	(508) 233-6753	Virginia	(434) 298-6222

Michigan	(517) 702-5120	Washington	(253) 512-8899
Minnesota	(651) 282-4508	West Virginia	(304) 561-6366
Mississippi	(601) 313-6300	Wisconsin	(608) 242-3447
Missouri	(573) 638-9500 x7746	Wyoming	(307) 772-5262

Courtesy of www.virtualarmory.com

REMEMBER: Each state has its own benefits for the National Guard. Research your own state's benefits and prepare to reap some significant educational opportunities!

CONCLUSION

Congratulations—You Did It! Now What?

"You are educated . . . you may think of it as the ticket to the good life. Let me ask you to think of an alternative. Think of it as your ticket to change the world!"

— Tom Brokaw

You Did It!

The hard part is done. You've obtained the certificate or degree you worked so hard for. It wasn't easy, but through determination and perseverance you have achieved your goals you set out to accomplish. Some of you had family, friends, and colleagues who offered support along the way. Never forget their reassurance and inspiration—or the added responsibilities they assumed so you could finish your educational goals. Be sure to offer them an opportunity to celebrate with you in some way. If you have the opportunity to attend a graduation ceremony—do so. Wear your cap and gown, shake the hand of your university representative, and feel that sense of pride that comes with knowing you've achieved something worthwhile. This is your time to shine and to bask in the glow of your accomplishments. You've earned it, so enjoy it.

The end of this journey, however, only means the beginning of another. After you take time to reflect on what you've accomplished, it will be time to take advantage of your new opportunities. Those of you who are currently employed may want to seek a promotion, and many of you may be looking forward to changing your career fields entirely.

If you are still in the military, consider obtaining that promotion you've been waiting for. Those of you who may have stalled on some boards may find that your degree enables you to finally get over the wall and progress to the next rank. You now hold an edge over much of your competition, and your degree gives you added value in the eyes of your supervisors. You are now an even more integral part of the team. Some of you may have ambitions to attend Warrant Officer or Officer Basic Course and make a transition in your career. Your bachelor's degree will put you near or at the front of the pack. Those of you close to retirement will have your degree in hand knowing that your military experience, coupled with your civilian education, will make you a prime candidate for civilian career opportunities.

Some of you may choose to do something completely different. Maybe your degree will help you start a new business or allow you to pursue a passion you've enjoyed thus far only as a hobby, but never had an opportunity to do because you were so busy with the rest of your life. Either way, be confident that your education will open new paths for you to explore and new opportunities to relish in.

Here's one option that some of you may be thinking about: Going *back* to school. We know what you are thinking. "After what I've been through, why would I want to go *back* to school?"

Continuing your education can <u>never</u> be the wrong idea. If you have earned a certificate, you should be considering how to obtain an associate's degree. If you have earned an associate's degree, you should be considering a bachelor's degree. If you have obtained a bachelor's degree, you should be considering a graduate degree or professional certification. Continuing your education even after you've completed a part of it should always be seen as another positive, helpful step in getting ahead in life.

Whether you move forward right away or take time off from school will depend upon your own personal circumstances. If your current certification or degree allows you to do so, by all means enjoy the fruits of your labor. Regardless of what you do, never stop thinking about how to continue your education. Some employers (and certainly the military) encourage you to continue school and even offer some financial incentive to do so. Take advantage of this opportunity with an advanced degree or certification and chances are, you'll be climbing the corporate ladder or moving up in the chain of command.

Lifelong Learning

Lifelong learning is the concept of continuing education throughout your adult life. For those of you who are or were in the service, think back about how wonderful it felt to graduate basic training and your occupation training. It was like climbing a mountain, right?

But what happened after that? You didn't just hit the battlefield and assume excellence. You were tested along the way, given refresher courses, studied, and given new and improved training. The constantly changing nature of the battlefield makes all this a requirement to excel. The American military would not be the dominent fighting force that it is today were it not for this constant studying and training.

The modern battlefield does not exist in a vacuum, and neither does life in the private sector. Take advantage of every learning opportunity that comes your way. Obtain that extra degree or certification to help you get that added edge—especially if someone else is paying for it!

Even if you decide not to pursue that additional degree or certification, take a refresher business or computer course at a local college from time to time. Keep your mind fresh and active, explore new things, and set new goals for yourself.

Your supervisors will appreciate this, and you will have the latest information to keep you competitive in the service or in the workplace.

These extra efforts will make you a valuable asset now and in the future.

NEVER STOP LEARNING.

Appendices

Checklist

Appendix 1 includes a checklist to help keep things in order as you conduct your research of schools, programs, and the application along the path to earn your degree.

Appendix 2 includes questions to ask admissions personnel.

CHECKLIST

This will help keep things in order as you conduct your research of schools, programs, and the application process. <u>Cut out and copy this checklist</u> as often as you need, and annotate it accordingly when doing your research.

Check When Complete	TASK — ACTION
	Determine the type of degree that you want to earn
	Figure out what type of student you are
	Conduct your research on 5 - 10 different colleges
	Request Information - include a request for specific information regarding your degree program
	Analyze your results
	Narrow your choices to 3 - 5 schools
	Inquire with each school
	Complete a Selection Checklist on each school
	Complete your Decision Matrix
	Analyze your results and make your decision
	Apply to the school
	Submit any required documents
	High School Transcripts
	Essays
	SAT / ACT / GMAT / GRE / LSAT Scores - If required
	College Transcripts for Transfer Credits
	Military Transcripts
	Resume

Check When Complete	TASK — ACTION
	Schedule a campus visit if planning on attending in a traditional mode
	Complete the FAFSA - www.fafsa.ed.org
	Complete your application or transfer of your GI Bill Benefits: http://vabenefits.vba.va.gove/vonapp/main.asp
	Complete your request for your Branch of Service Tuition Assistance
	Discuss your Transfer Evaluation with your Admissions Counselor or Academic Advisor
	When received, provide the Registrar's Office a copy of your VA Benefits Eligibility Notification
	When approved, provide your Admissions Counselor, Registrar, Financial Aid, or Bursar's Office a copy of your approved Tuition Assistance Notification
	When received, review your Financial Aid Award documents and return to the Financial Aid Office as indicated
	Complete the registration process as directed by your Admissions Counselor
	Order your books as instructed by your Admissions Counselor
	Complete any orientation programs as instructed by your Admissions Counselor
	Start your classes!
	Continually communicate with your Academic Advisor and Professors throughout your classes.

Appendix 2: Key questions

Place a +1 (plus 1) in the "Yes" column or a -1 (minus 1) in the "No" column. For the Bold questions, place either a + or – 3 (plus or minus 3), as these questions should be more heavily weighted. <u>Cut out and copy this checklist</u> as often as you need, and annotate it accordingly when doing your research.

Question	School:_____	YES	NO
Q-1	Is the school a member of SOC?		
Q-2	Is the school Nationally Accredited?		
Q-3	**Is the school Regionally Accredited?**		
Q-4	Is the school certified to receive GI Bill Benefits?		
Q-5	Is the school a Yellow Ribbon participating school?		
Q-6	**Does the school offer both traditional classes and online classes?**		
Q-7	If you attend as a traditional student, can you transfer to an online program without penalty?		
Q-8	**Can you have your military training and experience evaluated for college credits before enrolling as a student?**		
Q-9	Does the college offer a special tuition program for military students?		
Q-10	Does the college offer a special tuition program for veterans?		
Q-11	Does the college offer a special tuition program for military dependents?		

Question	School:_____	YES	NO
Q-12	Is there an application fee for military members, veterans, or military dependants?		
Q-13	Can you stay enrolled if you miss more than one term due to a military related requirement?		
Q-14	Does the school provide a waiver for the SCS on fees?		
Q-15	Does the school have experience in dealing with SCS students?		
Q-16	Does the school have a Veterans Affairs or similar office?		
Q-17	Does the school have a Career Services office that has experience in working with veterans and translating military training and experience into a viable resume?		
Q-18	Once you are ready to apply, can you do so in person and complete all required paperwork and, if required, placement testing during a scheduled campus visit?		
Q-19	**If you receive Tuition Assistance as a reimbursement, can you pay for your tuition once you receive your TA instead of paying upfront?**		
Q-20	**If you are ordered to active duty, does the school have a flexible withdrawal policy for military students?**		

DECISION MATRIX
(See completed sample on the following page)

Question	SCHOOL 1	SCHOOL 2	SCHOOL 3	SCHOOL 4	SCHOOL 5
SCHOOL NAME					
Q1					
Q2					
Q3					
Q4					
Q5					
Q6					
Q7					
Q8					
Q9					
Q10					
Q11					
Q12					
Q13					
Q14					
Q15					
Q16					
Q17					
Q18					
Q19					
Q20					
TOTAL					

Appendices: Checklist and Matrix 171

Question	SCHOOL 1	SCHOOL 2	SCHOOL 3	SCHOOL 4	SCHOOL 5
SCHOOL NAME					
Q1	+3	+3	+3	+3	+3
Q2	+1	+1	+1	+1	+1
Q3	+3	-3	+3	-3	+3
Q4	+1	+1	+1	-1	+1
Q5	+3	-3	-3	-3	-3
Q6	+3	-3	+3	-3	+3
Q7	+1	-1	+1	-1	-1
Q8	+3	+3	+3	-3	+3
Q9	+1	+1	+1	+1	+1
Q10	+1	+1	-1	+1	+1
Q11	+1	+1	-1	-1	+1
Q12	+1	+1	+1	-1	-1
Q13	+1	-1	+1	-1	-1
Q14	+1	+1	-1	-1	+1
Q15	+1	+1	+1	+1	+1
Q16	+1	-1	+1	-1	-1
Q17	+1	-1	+1	-1	-1
Q18	+1	+1	+1	-1	+1
Q19	+3	+3	+3	-3	+3
Q20	+3	+3	+3	+3	-3
TOTAL	+34	+8	+22	-14	+12

References

We utilized a wide variety of sources. Below are some of the major repositories of information we found the most useful when combined with our daily experience working in this area.

Clark, K. "How Much Is That College Degree Really Worth?" *U.S. News and World Report.* Retrieved from www.usnews.com/articles/education/ (October 30, 2008).

American Council on Education

Army American Council on Education Registry Transcript System

Community College of the Air Force

CollegeBoard.com

Columbia University

Department of Veterans Affairs

GoArmyEd

Military.com

Military One-Source

MilitaryTA.com

Post University

Sailor and Marine Council on Education Registry Transcript System

Index

Army/Ace Registry Transcript System, 23, 46, 75
academic advisor, 81
Accreditation, National, 42-43, 64
   Accrediting Commission of Career Schools and Colleges of Technology, 39
   Accrediting Council for Continuing Education and Training, 39
   Accrediting Council for Independent Colleges and Schools, 39
   Distance Education and Training Council, 39
Accreditation, Regional, 42-43
   Middle States Association of Colleges and Schools Middle States Commission on Higher Education (MSCHE), 40
   New England Association of Schools and Colleges Commission on Institutions of Higher Education (NEASC-CIHE), 40
   North Central Association of Colleges and Schools The Higher Learning Commission (NCA-HCL), 40
   Northwest Commission on Colleges and Universities (NWCCU), 41
   Southern Association of Colleges and Schools Commission on Colleges (SACS), 41
   Western Association of Schools and Colleges Accrediting Commission for Community and Junior Colleges (WASC-ACCJC), 41
   Western Association of Schools and Colleges Accrediting Commission for Senior Colleges and Universities (WASC-ACSCU), 41
Accrediting Commission of Career Schools and Colleges of Technology, 39
Accrediting Council for Continuing Education and Training, 39
Accrediting Council for Independent Colleges and Schools, 39
Active Duty for Special Work (ADSW), 156
Admissions Counselor, 36, 81
admissions process, 77, 81
aggregator site, 64
Air Force Reserve Office Training Corps, website, www.afrotc.com, 147
Air National Guard, 102, 155
American Council on Education (ACE), 23, 46; website, www.militaryguides.acenet.edu/showacecourses.asp?aceid=AR-2201-0253, 25
application fee, 64, 66
application process, 67
Army Reserve Officer Training Corps, website, www.goarmy.com/rotc, 147
Basic Allowance Housing (BAH), 100
Brokaw, Tom, quote, 160
Bryan, William Jennings, quote, 1

Career Advancement Accounts, 112-113; website, https://aiportal.acc.af.mil/mycaa, 113
career students, 55
career-oriented college degree, 18-21
Civilian Career Accounts, 87
College Admissions Process, 59, 62
college credits, 20-21
college degrees, career-oriented, 18-2; General Studies Degree, 18-20; Liberal Arts Degree, 18-20
College experience, the, 118
College Level Examination Program (CLEP), 26-28
College Loan Repayment Program (CLRP), 108, 110; eligibility, 109
Community and Junior Colleges, 57
Council of Higher Education Accreditation (CHEA), 40-41
credit bank, 43-44
Cumulative Grade Point Average, 115
DA-2171, 88
DD Form 149, Application for Correction of Military Records, 48
DD-214, 22, 53, 72, 75
Defense Activity for Non-Traditional Education Support (DANTES), 26-28
dependents, 102, 104-105
deployed students, 137-140, 153
diploma and degree mills, 42-43, 59
direct commission, 151
Disabled War Veteran Scholarship, 110
discounts, 6
Distance Education and Training Council, 39
distance learning, 115

education benefits, 8-10
Education Support Specialists (ESS), 17, 27
educational benefits, 69
Educational Support Offices (ESO), 27-28, 47, 56, 89, 90-91, 93, 113-114, 157; list of branches, 29-33; list of state ESO phone numbers, 158-159
Eisenhower, Gen. Dwight, 20
employer tuition reimbursement, 87
entrance exams, 78
Estimated Family Contribution (EFC), 69, 107-108
Facebook, 123
famous quotes; Brokaw, Tom, 160; Bryan, William Jennings, 1; Franklin, Benjamin, 86; King Jr., Dr. Martin Luther, 35; Lombardi, Vince, 129; Patton, Gen. George S., 117; Powell, Gen. Colin, 16; Rand, Ayn, 12; Roosevelt, Theodore, 61
Federal Financial Aid, 71, 106
Federal Pell Grant Program, 107-108
Federal Tuition Assistance Program (FTAP), 69, 71, 87, 94, 107, 153, 156
Form 22-1990, 105
Form 22-1995, 105
Franklin, Benjamin, quote, 86
Free Application For Federal Student Aid (FAFSA), 67, 71, 107-108; website, www.fafsa.ed.gov, 69
funding options, Federal Financial Aid, 71; MGIB-AD Chapter 30 benefit, 71; Top-Up Program, 71
General Studies Degree, 18-20
GI Bill Educational Benefits, 65, 104-105, 107, 109, 101, 113, 130-136, 146, 153, 156; post-9/11 GI Bill, 101; Yellow Ribbon Program,

101; dependents benefits, 104; post-9/11 GI Bill, 104; activating, 105
GoArmyEd/EArmyU, 81, 90-93
Grade Point Average (GPA), 78, 89, 115
Graduate Management Admissions Test (GMAT), 79
Graduate Readiness Exam (GRE), 78
grants, 6, 106-108
Green To Gold program, 146
immunization, 84
individual program requirements, 78
Institutions of Higher Education (IHE), 107
Intrepid Fallen Heroes Scholarships Fund, 110
Johnson, President Lyndon B., 94
King Jr., Dr. Martin Luther, quote, 35
Law School Admissions Test (LSAT), 79
letters of recommendation, 78
Liberal Arts college degree, 18-20
Lincoln, Abraham, 144
LinkedIn, 123
Lombardi, Vince, quote, 129
Low Residency Programs, 58
matriculation, 53, 79
merit-based scholarships, 69
Middle States Association of Colleges and Schools Middle States Commission on Higher Education (MSCHE), 40
Military Advanced Education (MAE), 47-48
military career as college credits, 20
military discounts, 115
Military Friendly School, 47-48
Military One Source; website, www.militaryonesource.com., 48
Military Scholar.com Scholarship Finder; website, www.militaryscholar.org, 111
Military Student Bill of Rights, 44-45
military universities, list of, 150
Military.com Scholarship Finder; http://aid.military.com/scholarship/search-for-scholarships.do, 111
Montgomery GI Bill, 13, 20, 39, 56-57, 62, 65, 87, 89, 94, 103, 156; Chapter 30, 71, 95; Category I, II and III, 96; Category IV, 97; Chapter 31, 97; Chapter 32, 97; Chapter 33, 98, 101, 105; Chapter 1606, 102, 104-105; Chapter 35, 102; Chapter 30, 105; website, www.gibill.va.gov/GI_Bill_Info/benefits.htm, 105
Morrill Land-Grant Colleges Act, 144
National EMT Registry, 21
National Guard, 89, 97, 102, 113-114, 128, 156; list of free tuition for, 157
Navy/Marine Reserve Officer Training Corps website, www.nrotc.navy.mil/, 147
need-based financial benefits, 69
networking, 121-128
New England Association of Schools and Colleges Commission on Institutions of Higher Education (NEASC-CIHE), 40
Night/Weekend Programs, 58
North Central Association of Colleges and Schools The Higher Learning Commission (NCA-HCL), 40
Northwest Commission on Colleges and Universities (NWCCU), 41

Office of Veterans Affairs (also, see Veterans Administration), 51
Officer Candidate School, 137, 141-143, 145-146
Official Transfer Evaluation, 67
online programs, 58, 115
Operation Enduring Freedom, 110
Operation Iraqi Freedom, 110
Parent loan, 106, 108
Patton, Gen. George S., quote, 117
pay-grade requirements, 88
Powell, Gen. Colin, quote, 16
prerequisites, 81
private schools, 57
Rand, Ayn, quote, 12
registration, 79-80
reserve branches websites
   Air Force Reserves, www.afreserve.com, 155
   Army Reserves, www.usar.army.mil/arweb.pages.default.aspx, 155
   Coast Guard Reserves, www.uscg.mil/reserve, 155
   Marine Reserves, www.marforres.usmc.mil/, 155
   Navy Reserves, www.navyreserve.com, 155
Reserve Officer Training Corps, 143-147, 149, 152
Reserve Officer Training Corps Scholarships, 110
reserves, 153-154, 157
resident student, 69
resumes, 78
Roosevelt, President Franklin D., 94
Roosevelt, Theodore, quote, 61
Satisfactory Academic Progress, 115
scholarships, 6, 110-111; definition, 7; Disabled War Veteran Scholarship, 110; Intrepid Fallen Heroes Scholarships Fund, 110; Military Scholar.com Scholarship, www.militaryscholar.org, 111; Military.com Scholarship, http://aid.military.com/scholarship/search-for-scholarships.do, 111; ROTC Scholarships, 110, 145; Tillman Military Scholar- ships, 110
Selected Reserve Montgomery GI Bill, tuition assistance, 103; website, www.gibill.va.gov/GI_Bill_Info/benefits.htm, 102
service academies
   United States Air Force Academy, 148
   United States Coast Guard Academy, 149
   United States Merchant Marine Academy, 149
   United States Military Academy, 149
   United States Naval Academy, 149
Service Connected Students (SCS), vi, viii-ix, 6, 13, 26, 28, 44, 48, 59, 62, 72, 107; definition, 6, 8-10; challenges, 17; decision on a degree plan, 17-18; Career-oriented college degree, 20; twenty questions, 36-38; military friendly school, 47; support from colleges, 49-50; changing schools, 51-52, 54, 56; matric- ulation, 53, 79; career students, 55; changing a degree program, 55; academic goals, 60; college admissions, 63; educational benefits, 69; registration, 71, 77, 79-80; transcripts, 77-78; transfer students, 77, 80; entrance exams, 78; GoArmyEd/EArmyU, 81,

Index 177

91-93; admissions process, 82, 85; tuition assistance, 87, 90-91, 93, 130-136; Federal Tuition Assistance Program (FTAP), 94; Montgomery GI Bill, 98-99; Yellow Ribbon Program, 101; Survivors and Dependents' Education Assistance Program, 102; scholarships, 110-111; military discounts, 115; the college experience, 118-120; networking, 121-128; importance of having a degree, 136; deployment, 138-140; Officer Candidate School, 141-143; ROTC, 143-147; Green To Gold program, 146; direct commission, 151

service-connected disabilities, 97

Serviceman's Readjustment Act of 1944, 94

Servicemembers Opportunity College (SOC), 44-46, 65

Southern Association of Colleges and Schools Commission on Colleges (SACS), 41

spouse tuition assistance
    Air Force Spouse Tuition Assistance Program (STAP), 112
    Army Overseas Spouse Assistance Program (OSEAP), 112
    Army Stateside Spouse Education Assistance Program (SEAP), 112
    Marine Corps and Navy Spouse Tuition Aid Program (STAP), 112

Stafford Student Loans, 107-108

State Colleges and Universities, 57

State Education Officer, 89

State Military Grant, 156

State Tuition Waiver, 156

stipends, 6

Student Loan Repayment plans, 130-136, 156

Student Plus loan, 106, 108

support from colleges and universities: Academic Advising, 49; Academic Advising, 50; Career Services, 49; Career Services, 50; Financial Aid Services, 49; Library Services and Research Assistance, 49; Tutoring Services, 49; Veteran's Affairs and Assistance, 49

Survivors and Dependents' Education Assistance Program, 102; website, www.gibill.va.gov/GI_Bill_Info/benefits.htm, 102

Technical/Trade Schools, 57

Tillman Military Scholarships, 110

Title IV Federal Financial Aid, 65, 87, 106-108, 115

Top-Up Program, 71, 95

Traditional Programs, 58

transcripts, 67, 77-78

transfer students, 77, 80

Troops-to-Teachers program, 19

tuition assistance, 81, 88, 90, 92, 103, 105, 113, 130-136, 156; Civilian Career Accounts, 87; employer tuition reimbursement, 87; Federal Tuition Assistance Program (FTAP), 87; Montgomery GI Bill, 87, 89; Title IV Federal Financial Aid, 87; electronic applications, 90; website, United States Coast Guard, www.yscg.mil/HQ/CGI/cfa/ta.asp, 90; United States Marines/Navy, www.navycollege.Navy.mil.nta.cfm, 90; National Guard, www.virtualarmory.com/education/fedbenefits/tuition_fta.aspx, 90; United States Air Force, www.my.af.mil/ 93; GoArmyEd/ EArmyU, 93; Chapter 1606, 102; Federal Pell Grant, 107-108; Stafford Student Loans, 107-108, Disabled War Veteran Scholarship, 110; Intrepid Fallen Heroes Scholarships Fund, 110; ROTC Scholarships, 110; scholarships, 110; Tillman Military Scholarships, 110; Military Scholar.com Scholarship Finder, 112; Military.com Scholarship Finder, 112; states offering free tuition for veterans, 113; distance learning, 115; military discounts, 115; Online Programs, 115

Types of programs: Low residency Programs, 58; Night/Weekend Programs, 58; Online Programs, 58; Traditional Programs, 58

U.S. Department of Education (USDE), 39-40, 106

U.S. News and World Report, 6-7

United States Air Force Academy, 148-149; website,
www.usafa.af.mil/, 149

United States Coast Guard Academy, 149; website,
www.cga.edu, 149

United States Merchant Marine Academy, 149; website,
www.usmma.edu, 149

United States Military Academy, 147, 149; website,
www.usma.edu, 149

United States Naval Academy, 149, website,
www.usna.edu, 149

USC Title 32 AG/R, 97

variety of schools, Community and Junior Colleges, 57; private schools, 57; State Colleges and Universities, 57; Technical/Trade Schools, 57

Verification of Military and Training, 49, website,
www.dmdc.osd.mil/appj/vmet/logindisplay.do., 48

Veterans Administration (VA), 62-63, 84, 95, 97, 100; website, www.defensetravel.dod.mil/perdiem/bah.html, 100; website, www.gibill.va.gov/GI_Bill_Info/benefits.htm#CH33, 101; change of benefits, 104-105; website, www.gibill.va.gov/GI_Bill_Info/benefits.htm, 104; Veterans Online Application System, 105; states offering free tuition for veterans, 113

Veterans Education Assistance program (VEAP), 97

Veterans Online Application System, 105; website,
www.vabenefits.vba.va.gov/vonapp/main.asp, 105

Veteran's Readjustment Benefits Act of 1966, 94

Vocational Rehabilitation component, 97

waivers, 6

Warrant Officer Candidate School (WOCS), 161; websites
Army,
www.usawocc.army.mil/, 152
Coast Guard,
www.cga.edu.ldc_display.aspx?id=652, 152
Marines,
www.marines.mil/units/hqmc/pages/default.aspx, 152
Navy,
www.ocs.navy.mil/ldo_program_overview.asp, 152

Western Association of Schools and Colleges Accrediting Commission for Community and Junior Colleges (WASC-ACCJC), 41

Western Association of Schools and Colleges Accrediting Commission for Senior Colleges and Universities (WASC-ACSCU), 41

Yellow Ribbon Program, 101; website, www.gibill.va.gov/GI_Bill_Info/CH33/YRP/YRP_List.htm, 101

Websites
(in the order of appearance)

Troops-to-Teachers: www.proudtoserveagain.com, 19 (transcript for military training)
Air Force/ANG: www.au.af.mil/au/ccaf/, 22
Army/ANG: https://aartstranscript.army.mil/, 22
Coast Guard: www.uscg.mil/hq/cgi/ve/official_transcript.asp, 22
Marines/Navy: https://smart.navy.mil/smart/dod, 22
American Council on Education (ACE): www.militaryguides.acenet.edu/showacecourses.asp?aceid=AR-2201-0253, 25
Military One Source: www.militaryonesource.com, 48
Verification of Military and Training: www.dmdc.osd.mil/appj/vmet/logindisplay.do, 48
Free Application For Federal Student Aid (FAFSA): www.fafsa.ed.gov, 69
Coast Guard: www.uscg.mil/HQ/CGI/cfa/ta.asp, 90
Marines/Navy: www.navycollege.navy.mil/nta.cfm, 90
National Guard: www.virtualarmory.com/education/fedbenefits/tuition/fta.aspx, 90
Air Force: www.my.af.mil/, 93
Veterans Administration: www.defensetravel.dod.mil/perdiem/bah.htm, 100
GI Bill: www.gibill.va.gov/GI_Bill_Info/benefits.htm#CH33, 101
Cchange of benefits: www.gibill.va.gov/GI_Bill_Info/benefits.htm, 104, 105
Veterans Online Application System: www.vabenefits.vba.va.gov/vonapp/
main.asp, 105
GI Bill, Yellow Ribbon Program: wwwgibill.va.gov/GI_Bill_Info/CH33/YRP/YRP_List.htm, 101
Survivors and Dependents' Education Assistance Program: www.gibill.va.gov/GI_Bill_Info/benefits.htm, 102
Selected Reserve Montgomery GI Bill: www.gibill.va.gove/GI_Bill_Info/benefits.htm, 103
Military Scholar.com Scholarship Finder: www.militaryscholar.org, 111

Military.com Scholarship Finder: http://aid.military.com/scholarship/search-for-scholarships.do, 111

Career Advancement Accounts: https://aiportal.acc.af.mil/mycaa, 113

Air Force ROTC: www.afrotc.com, 147

Army ROTC: www.goarmy.com/rotc, 147

Navy/Marine ROTC: www.nrotc.navy.mil/, 147

United States Air Force Academy: www.usafa.af.mil/, 149

United States Coast Guard Academy: www.cga.edu, 149

United States Merchant Marine Academy: www.usmma.edu, 149

United States Military Academy: www.usma.edu, 149

United States Naval Academy: www.usna.edu, 149

Army Warrant Officer: www.usawocc.army.mil/, 152

Coast Guard Warrant Officer: www.cga.edu.ldc_display.aspx?id=652, 152

Marine Warrant Officer, www.marines.mil/units/hqmc/pages/default.aspx, 152

Navy Warrant Officer: www.ocs.navy.mil/ldo_program_overview.asp, 152

Air Force Reserves: www.afreserve.com, 155

Army Reserves: www.usar.army.mil/arweb.pages.default.aspx, 155

Coast Guard Reserves: www.uscg.mil/reserve, 155

Marine Reserves: www.marforres.usmc.mil/, 155

Navy Reserves: www.navyreserve.com, 155

About the Authors

David J. Renza is a U.S. Army veteran who served in the Connecticut Army National Guard for twelve years. As a combat medic, he was deployed to Bosnia and Herzegovina after September 11, 2001. He is a three-time winner of the Army Achievement Medal and a recipient of the Army Commendation Medal for his work as a retention NCO. Renza holds a Master's of Arts from the University of Connecticut's Neag School of Education. He is currently a Military Enrollment Counselor with Post University.

Lt. Col. Edmund J. Lizotte is a U.S. Army veteran with 25 years of service. He has held various positions throughout his career, from platoon and scout platoon leader to battalion and brigade operations officer. Lizotte has received two Meritorious Service medals, five Army Commendation medals, and four Army Achievement medals. He holds a Bachelor's of Science from the University of Massachusetts and is a graduate of both the Combined Arms Staff and Services School and the Army Command and General Staff College. He currently serves as the Director of Military Programs at Post University.